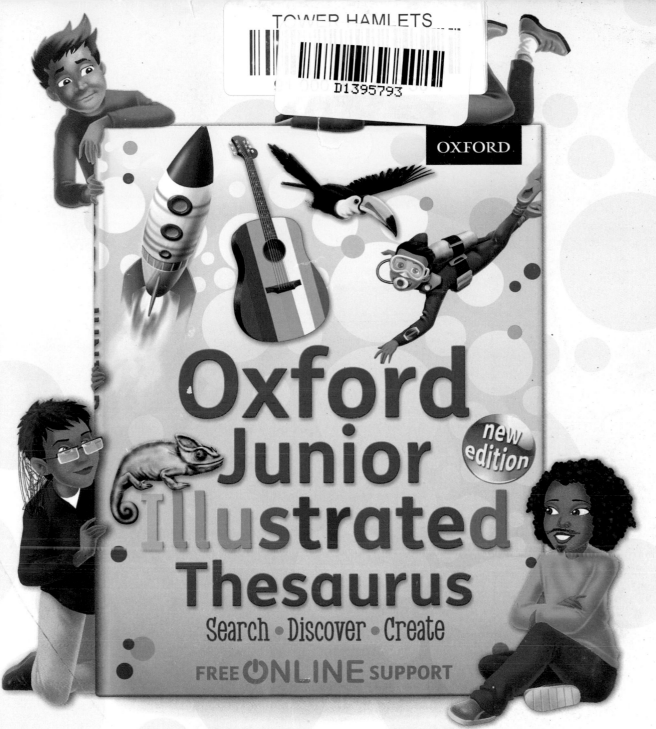

OXFORD

Oxford Junior Illustrated Thesaurus

new edition

Search • Discover • Create

FREE ONLINE SUPPORT

Editors: Sheila Dignen and Morven Dooner
Literacy Consultant: Kate Ruttle

OXFORD
UNIVERSITY PRESS

OXFORD
UNIVERSITY PRESS

Great Clarendon Street, Oxford OX2 6DP

Oxford University Press is a department of the University of Oxford.
It furthers the University's objective of excellence in research, scholarship,
and education by publishing worldwide in

Oxford New York

Auckland Cape Town Dar es Salaam Hong Kong Karachi
Kuala Lumpur Madrid Melbourne Mexico City Nairobi
New Delhi Shanghai Taipei Toronto

With offices in
Argentina Austria Brazil Chile Czech Republic France Greece
Guatemala Hungary Italy Japan Poland Portugal Singapore
South Korea Switzerland Thailand Turkey Ukraine Vietnam

© Oxford University Press 2012

Database right Oxford University Press (maker)

First published 2003
New edition 2007
This new edition 2012

Artwork by Dynamo Design Ltd.
Photos: Pages 15, 20, 134, 182 and 211 © iStockphoto/Thinkstock
Pages 17 and 157 © Goodshoot/Thinkstock : Pages 24, 60, 103 and 123 © Hemera/Thinkstock
Pages 26 and 162 © Comstock/Thinkstock : Page 30 © photos.com/Thinkstock
Page 65 © Stockbyte/Thinkstock : Pages 76 and 208-209 © Photos to Go
Pages 82 and 124 © Rex Features : Page 131 © Ryan McVay/Lifesize/Thinkstock
Pages 132-133 © John Snelling/Rex Features : Page 193 © Linda Wright/Science Photo Library
Page 217 © George Doyle/Stockbyte/Thinkstock

British Library Cataloguing in Publication Data available

ISBN hardback 978-0-19-275685-5
ISBN paperback 978-0-19-275686-2

10 9 8 7 6 5 4 3 2 1

Printed in Printed in Malaysia

Paper used in the production of this book is a natural,
recyclable product made from wood grown in sustainable
forests. The manufacturing process conforms to the
environmental regulations of the country of origin.

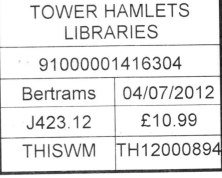

TEACHERS
For inspirational support plus
free resources and eBooks
www.oxfordprimary.co.uk

PARENTS
Help your child's reading
with essential tips, phonics
support and free eBooks
www.oxfordowl.co.uk

Contents

Preface

Discover the power of words with this new edition of the **Oxford Junior Illustrated Thesaurus**. The pages are contemporary, bright, and colourful which makes it easy to find the words you need. The text has been specially written for primary school children aged 7-9 years, has been created using the Oxford Children's Corpus, and tested in the classroom with teachers and children. The headwords have been carefully chosen and are words that children are most likely to look up, and the synonyms and alternative words are a mixture of familiar and unfamiliar words that will stretch children's vocabulary. At the back of the book is an indispensable guide for creative writing and effective use of English.

If you love learning about new words and language, and want to find synonyms for words that are not in this thesaurus, try a bigger thesaurus, for example, the Oxford Primary Thesaurus.

www.oxforddictionaries.com/schools

Introduction

What is the difference between a thesaurus and a dictionary?

A **dictionary** tells you what a word means, so it gives you a **definition** of the word.

A **thesaurus** tells you what other words have the same meaning, so it gives you **synonyms** of a word.

You use a dictionary when you have read, or heard, a new word and want to know what it means. You use a thesaurus when you want to write or say something yourself and you want to choose the best word.

Here are some good reasons why you should use a thesaurus:

- **to find a more interesting word** Are there any alternative words to describe clothes that are very **dirty**? Look up **dirty** to find some other adjectives to describe dirty clothes.

- **to find the right word** What word might you use to describe **rain**? Look up **rain** to find the right word.

- **to make your writing more interesting** Instead of saying that someone ate a whole pizza, you might write: He **wolfed** down a whole pizza! or He **polished** off a whole pizza!

Synonyms are words that mean the same—or nearly the same—as each other. You can make your writing more interesting by using different synonyms, rather than using the same words all the time.

Imagine you are writing about what you did at the weekend. You might start like this:

> *I had a good weekend. The weather was not very nice so we went to the shops. I got a new top that is really nice. I met up with my friend and we went to see a film. I thought it was good but my friend didn't like it.*

Can you see that the words **nice** and **good** are used over and over again? If you look up these words in this thesaurus, you will find a number of synonyms with a similar meaning.

> *I had a **brilliant** weekend. The weather was not very **sunny** so we went to the shops. I got a new top and it is really **stylish**. I met up with my friend and we went to see a film. I thought it was **amusing** but my friend didn't like it.*

How to use this thesaurus

alphabet
on every page the alphabet is divided into four sections, with the letter you are in highlighted, so you can find your way around quickly and easily

opposite (antonym)
words that have an opposite meaning to the headword

writing tips panel
sentences and words, with examples taken from the best children's writers, to inspire you to write creatively

headword
in blue, it is the word you look up and is in alphabetical order

word class
what type of word it is, for example, noun, verb, adjective, or adverb

synonyms
words that mean the same, or nearly the same as the headword

other forms
unusual forms are given in full

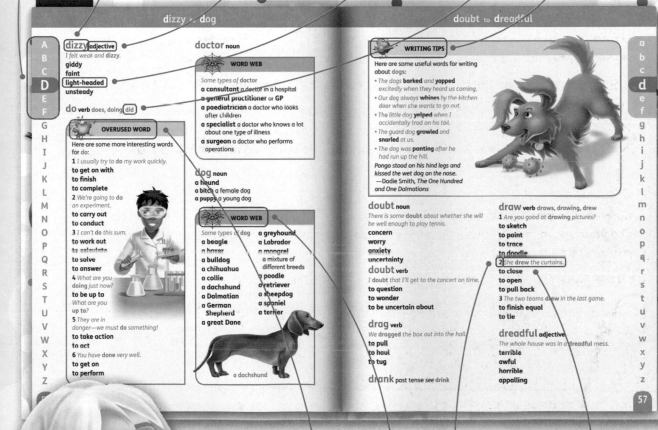

overused word panel
lots of alternatives for words that are used over and over again

numbered sense
if a word has more than one meaning, they are numbered

example sentence
shows how the word is used—this helps you choose a synonym for the right meaning

word web panel
words that are related to the headword or are types of the headword

Writing tips

The panels in this thesaurus give you extra help choosing the best word to use. There are three kinds of panels. **Look for the icons!**

WRITING TIPS

OVERUSED WORDS

WORD WEB

You will find **WRITING TIPS** at these entries:

aircraft	boat	dog	light	river
bell	car	horse	monster	water
bird	cat	insect	rain	wind

The **Writing tips** include words and sentences to show you ways of writing about the headword. For example, the **Writing tip** at **insect** shows how you can use words such as **buzz**, **crawl**, **scuttle** and **scurry** when you are writing about insects.

insect noun

 WRITING TIPS

Here are some useful words for writing about **insects**:
- *The ladybird* **flew** *away.*
- *A wasp was* **buzzing** *around the kitchen.*
- *Bees come together and* **swarm** *when they are looking for a new hive.*
- *A fly* **crawled** *up my leg.*
- *The beetle* **scuttled** *away.*
- *Ants were* **scurrying** *around looking for food.*

Insects were swarming all over the earthen mound inside the container.
—Jan Henderson, *Colony*

Overused words

You will find **OVERUSED WORDS** at these entries:

bad	eat	good	look	old	say
beautiful	get	happy	lovely	put	small
big	give	hard	move	run	strong
bit	go	little	nice	sad	walk
do					

When you are writing, look out for words that you use over and over again. Look them up in this thesaurus and you will find lots of more interesting synonyms.

For example, look at this postcard. The words **nice** and **good** are **Overused words** because they are used over and over again. We can make this postcard more interesting if we use a different adjective each time.

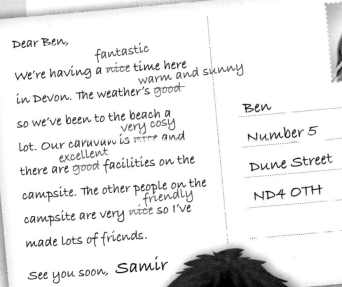

Dear Ben,

We're having a ~~nice~~ *fantastic* time here in Devon. The weather's ~~good~~ *warm and sunny* so we've been to the beach a lot. Our caravan is ~~nice~~ *very cosy* and there are ~~good~~ *excellent* facilities on the campsite. The other people on the campsite are very ~~nice~~ *friendly* so I've made lots of friends.

See you soon, Samir

Ben

Number 5

Dune Street

ND4 0TH

beautiful adjective

> **OVERUSED WORD**
>
> Here are some more interesting words for **beautiful**:
>
> **1** *He married the **beautiful** princess.*
> **lovely**
> **pretty**
> **fair**
> **attractive**
> Use **gorgeous** or **stunning** if someone is very beautiful: *You look absolutely **stunning** in that dress!*
>
> Use **glamorous** if someone looks beautiful and rich: *She looked like a **glamorous** actress.*
> OPPOSITE **ugly**
>
> **2** *The weather was **beautiful** for sports day.*
> **lovely**
> **gorgeous**
> **wonderful**
> **fantastic**
> **fine**
> OPPOSITE **awful**

Word webs

You will find **WORD WEB** panels at these entries:

aircraft	cage	dog	light	shop
animal	car	farm	material	song
bag	cat	film	meal	sound
bat	chair	flower	monster	sport
bed	clock	fruit	music	story
bicycle	clothes	hair	picture	tool
bird	colour	hat	plant	tree
boat	computer	horse	poem	vegetable
body	cook	house	religion	writer
book	cup	insect	seat	
bridge	dance	jewel	shape	
building	doctor	job	shoe	

Some words are not synonyms, but are related because they have similar meanings to your word.

For example, **flower** is a general word, which can mean any type of flower. The words **rose**, **daffodil**, and **tulip** are related because they describe one specific type of flower. It can help your reader to 'see' what you are writing about if you use more specific words.

Example:

Instead of saying that a garden is full of **flowers**, you might write:

*The garden was full of brightly-coloured **lilies** and sweet-smelling **roses**.*

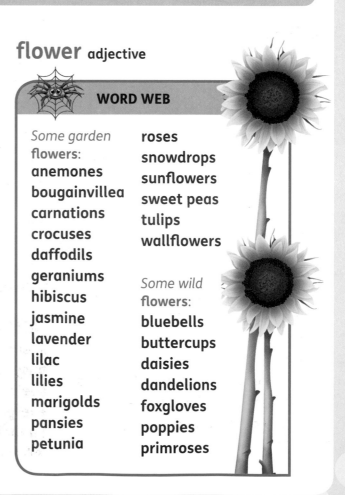

flower adjective

WORD WEB

Some garden flowers:
anemones
bougainvillea
carnations
crocuses
daffodils
geraniums
hibiscus
jasmine
lavender
lilac
lilies
marigolds
pansies
petunia
roses
snowdrops
sunflowers
sweet peas
tulips
wallflowers

Some wild flowers:
bluebells
buttercups
daisies
dandelions
foxgloves
poppies
primroses

Aa

ability noun
1 *You are clever and have the **ability** to do well at school.*
capability
intelligence
2 *He's a young footballer with a lot of **ability** for the game.*
talent
skill
flair

about adverb
*There are **about** 30 children in our class.*
roughly
approximately

accept verb
*The children stepped forward to **accept** the prizes from the teachers.*
to take
to receive
OPPOSITE **reject**

accident noun
1 *There was a nasty **accident** on the road.*
a crash
a smash
a collision
A **pile-up** is a bad accident with a lot of cars.
A **bump** is an accident that is not very bad.
2 *I'm sorry, it was an **accident**.*
a mistake

achieve verb
*You have **achieved** a lot this term.*
to do
to accomplish

achievement noun
*Winning a gold medal is a great **achievement**.*
an accomplishment
a feat
a success

act verb
1 *We must **act** quickly if we want tickets for the concert.*
to do something
to take action
2 *I would love to **act** on the stage.*
to perform
to appear

action noun
1 *I like films that are full of **action** as they are exciting.*
excitement
suspense
2 *His brave **action** saved his sister's life.*
an act
a deed

active adjective
*Most children enjoy playing and being **active**.*
busy
lively
energetic
on the go (informal)
OPPOSITE **inactive**

A
B
C
D
E
F
G
H
I
J
K
L
M
N
O
P
Q
R
S
T
U
V
W
X
Y
Z

activity noun
What activities do you do outside school?
a hobby
a pastime
an interest

actual adjective
This is the actual ship that Nelson sailed on.
real
genuine
very

add verb
Mix the butter and sugar together, then add the eggs.
to mix in

admire verb
1 *Which sports stars do you admire?*
to respect
to look up to
to idolize
to hero-worship
2 *We stood and admired the lovely view of the mountains.*
to enjoy
to appreciate

admit verb
He admitted that he had broken the window.
to confess
to own up
OPPOSITE **deny**

adult noun
You must be accompanied by an adult at all times.
a grown-up

adventure noun
He told us about all his exciting adventures.
an escapade
an exploit

advice noun
He gave me some very useful advice.
help
guidance
a suggestion *He made a useful suggestion.*

aeroplane noun
The aeroplane flew over the mountains.
a plane
an aircraft

afraid adjective
1 *Are you afraid of spiders?*
frightened
scared
Use **terrified** or **petrified** if you are very afraid: *I'm absolutely terrified of snakes.*

2 *I was afraid the boat might capsize.*
worried
nervous

aim verb
He aimed his water pistol at his aunt.
to point

aircraft noun

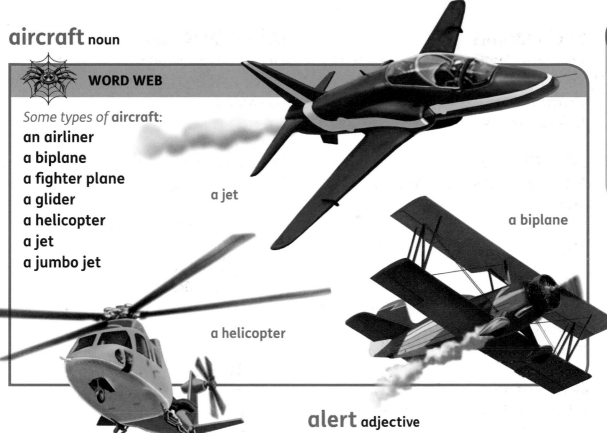

WORD WEB

Some types of **aircraft**:
an airliner
a biplane
a fighter plane
a glider
a helicopter
a jet
a jumbo jet

a jet

a biplane

a helicopter

WRITING TIPS

Here are some useful words for writing about **aircraft**:
• *The aircraft was* **flying** *above the clouds.*
• *The jumbo jet* **soared** *up into the sky.*
• *Our plane* **took off** *at six o'clock and landed at ten o'clock.*
The aircraft stayed very low, following the coastline. — David Miller, Shark Island

alarm noun

The fire **alarm** *went off noisily.*
a signal
a siren

alert adjective

The sentries on duty must remain **alert**.
ready
awake
on the lookout

alive adjective

The bird was injured but still **alive**.
living
breathing
OPPOSITE **dead**

allow verb

They **allowed** *us to use their swimming pool.*
to let *They* **let** *us use their swimming pool.*
to permit *They* **permitted** *us to use the swimming pool.*
to give someone permission *They* **gave us permission** *to use the swimming pool.*
OPPOSITE **forbid**

A
B
C
D
E
F
G
H
I
J
K
L
M
N
O
P
Q
R
S
T
U
V
W
X
Y
Z

all right adjective

1 *Were you all right after the accident?*
well
safe
unhurt
healthy
2 *The food in the restaurant was all right, but not brilliant.*
OK
acceptable
satisfactory

almost adverb

I've almost finished making dinner so we can eat soon.
nearly
virtually
practically

amaze verb

The entertainer at the party amazed us with his magic tricks.
to astonish
to astound

amazed adjective

I was amazed when I saw his new mountain bike.
astonished
staggered
flabbergasted *(informal)*
stunned

amazing adjective

What an amazing car!
wonderful
fantastic
incredible

amount noun

They ate a huge amount of food at the party!
a quantity

amuse verb

His jokes amused us all.
to entertain
to make someone laugh

amusing adjective

He told us a very amusing story.
funny
humorous
entertaining

anger noun

She couldn't hide her anger.
annoyance
Use **irritation** for slight anger: *He waved the flies away in irritation.*

Use **fury** or **rage** for very great anger: *Mr Evans turned crimson with rage.*

angry adjective

Mum looked very angry.
cross
annoyed
mad *(informal)*
Use **irritated** if someone is slightly angry: *My mum gets a bit irritated if I keep asking her questions.*

Use **furious** or **livid** if someone is very angry: *My dad was absolutely livid when he saw what we'd done.*

animal noun

*My cat is a very loving **animal**.*

a creature

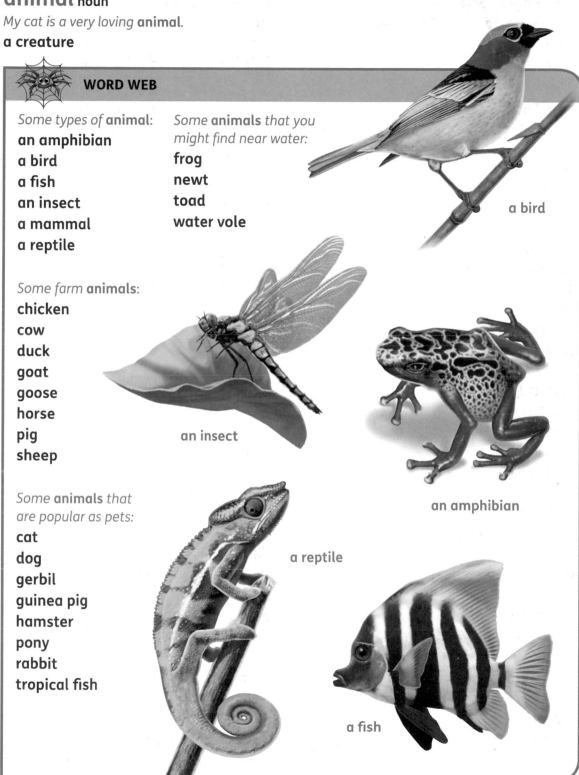

🕷 WORD WEB

*Some types of **animal**:*
an amphibian
a bird
a fish
an insect
a mammal
a reptile

*Some **animals** that you might find near water:*
frog
newt
toad
water vole

a bird

*Some farm **animals**:*
chicken
cow
duck
goat
goose
horse
pig
sheep

an insect

an amphibian

*Some **animals** that are popular as pets:*
cat
dog
gerbil
guinea pig
hamster
pony
rabbit
tropical fish

a reptile

a fish

a b c d e f g h i j k l m n o p q r s t u v w x y z

A
B
C
D
E
F
G
H
I
J
K
L
M
N
O
P
Q
R
S
T
U
V
W
X
Y
Z

WORD WEB

Some wild animals you might see in Britain:

badger
deer
fox
hare
hedgehog
mole
mouse
pinemartin
rabbit
rat
shrew
squirrel

Some other wild animals:

baboon
camel
cheetah
chimpanzee
crocodile
elephant
gazelle
giraffe
gorilla
hippopotamus
leopard
lion
monkey

panther
penguin
rhinoceros
tiger
zebra

Collective nouns for some groups of animals:

a flock of birds
a flock of sheep

a gaggle of geese
a herd of cattle
a litter of puppies
a pack of wolves
a pride of lions
a school of whales
a shoal of fish
a swarm of bees

a lion

a lioness

a giraffe

a rhinoceros

6

annoy verb
1 *The loud music was* **annoying** *me.*
to irritate
to get on someone's nerves
2 *My little brother keeps* **annoying** *me!*
to pester
to bother
to tease
to bug
OPPOSITE **please**

annoying adjective
Sometimes my sister can be very **annoying**.
irritating
tiresome
exasperating

answer noun
I called his name, but there was no **answer**.
a reply
a response

answer verb
I shouted to her, but she didn't **answer**.
to reply
to respond

apologize verb
I **apologized** *to my grandmother for being so rude.*
to say sorry

appear verb
The ship **appeared** *on the horizon.*
to arrive
to come into view
to become visible
OPPOSITE **disappear**

approach verb
I started to feel nervous as we **approached** *the theatre.*
to come near to
to come towards

area noun
1 *There is a special* **area** *where you can play.*
a place
a space
a patch
2 *This is a very nice* **area** *of the city.*
a part
a district

argue verb
The children were **arguing** *over the toys.*
to quarrel
to squabble
to fight
to fall out
To **bicker** means to argue about small things that are not important: *The two girls were bickering about whose pencil it was.*
OPPOSITE **agree**

argument noun
They had a big **argument** *over whose house they would go to.*
a quarrel
a disagreement
a row
a fight

arrange verb
1 *She* **arranged** *the books carefully on the shelf.*
to place
to set out

a
b
c
d
e
f
g
h
i
j
k
l
m
n
o
p
q
r
s
t
u
v
w
x
y
z

A
B
C
D
E
F
G
H
I
J
K
L
M
N
O
P
Q
R
S
T
U
V
W
X
Y
Z

2 *We have* **arranged** *to meet at ten o'clock.*

to plan

to agree

3 *My mother has* **arranged** *everything for my party.*

to organize

to plan

arrive verb

1 *We finally* **arrived** *in London.*

to reach

to get to

2 *Jessica* **arrived** *at the party two hours late.*

to come

to turn up

3 *When does the plane* **arrive** *in New York?*

to land

to touch down

to get in

4 *The boat should* **arrive** *at ten o'clock.*

to dock

to get in

OPPOSITE **depart**

art noun

I really enjoy doing **art** *at school.*

drawing

painting

sketching

modelling

pottery

sculpture

graphics

ask verb

He **asked** *me what my name was.*

to enquire

ask for

I've **asked for** *a new bike for my birthday.*

to request

To **demand** something means to say that you must have it: *He held out his hand and* **demanded** *the money.*

To **beg** for something means to ask someone very strongly for it: *'Please, please can I go?' she* **begged.**

asleep adjective

Grandfather was **asleep** *in front of the fire.*

sleeping

dozing

resting

slumbering

snoozing

having a nap

OPPOSITE **awake**

astonish verb

She **astonished** *us with her skilful tricks.*

to amaze

to astound

astonished adjective

I was **astonished** *when he told me how much his bike cost.*

amazed

staggered

flabbergasted

stunned

ate verb past tense see **eat**

athlete noun

They are very talented **athletes.**

a sportsman

a sportswoman

a runner
a sprinter
a high jumper
a long jumper

athletics noun

She is very good at athletics, especially running.

running
sprinting
hurdles
high jump
long jump
triple jump
cross-country
marathon
relay race

attach verb

You must attach the string firmly to the kite.

to fix
to fasten
to join
to connect
to tie
to stick
to glue

attack verb

The two robbers attacked them.

to assault
to set upon

To **ambush** someone means to jump out from a hiding place and attack them: *Robbers hide in the hills and ambush travellers.*

To **mug** someone means to attack and rob them in the street: *Two men tried to mug an old lady in the street.*

attractive adjective

1 *She's a very attractive girl.*
beautiful
pretty
lovely
gorgeous
2 *He's an attractive boy.*
handsome
good-looking
OPPOSITE unattractive

avoid verb

1 *I'm allergic to cats, so I try to avoid them.*
to keep away from
to steer clear of
2 *He always tries to avoid doing the washing up.*
to get out of

award noun

He got a special award for his bravery.
a prize
a reward
a trophy
a cup
a medal

awful adjective

What an awful smell!
terrible
dreadful
horrible

awkward adjective

1 *The box was an awkward shape.*
difficult
bulky
2 *They arrived at a very awkward time.*
inconvenient

a b c d e f g h i j k l m n o p q r s t u v w x y z

Bb

baby noun
a child
an infant
A **toddler** is a baby that is just learning to walk.

back noun
1 *We sat at the **back** of the hall.*
the rear
2 *I was at the **back** of the bus.*
the end
the rear
OPPOSITE **front**

bad adjective

OVERUSED WORD

Here are some more interesting words for **bad**:

1 *He's a **bad** man.*

Use **wicked** for a very bad person: *The country was ruled by a **wicked** king.*

Use **evil** for something that is very bad and frightening: *I sensed that there was something **evil** in that cave.*

Use **cruel** for someone who is very unkind and enjoys hurting people: *The two horses were bought by a **cruel** master who did not treat them well.*

Use **nasty** for someone who is mean or unkind: *He's a mean and **nasty** boy!*

2 *You **bad** dog!*

Use **naughty** or **disobedient** for a person or animal who doesn't do as they are told: *He was a very **naughty** dog who did not do as he was told.*

3 *There has been a **bad** accident and people have been hurt.*
terrible
awful
dreadful
horrible
shocking

4 *I'm very **bad** at maths.*
hopeless
useless
poor
terrible
weak
incompetent

5 *Sarah's got a **bad** knee.*
sore
injured
painful

6 *Food goes **bad** if you don't keep it in the fridge.*

Use **off** for meat and fish: *Don't eat the meat as it has gone **off**.*

Use **sour** for milk or cream: *This milk has gone **sour**.*

Use **mouldy** for cheese: *The cheese was **mouldy** and smelly.*

Use **rotten** for fruit: *The apples were brown and **rotten**.*
OPPOSITE **good**

bag noun

*She packed her books into her **bag**.*

*Some types of **bag**:*

- a **backpack**
- a **briefcase**
- a **carrier bag**
- a **handbag**
- a **holdall**
- a **rucksack**
- a **school bag**
- a **satchel**
- a **suitcase**
- a **trunk**

a rucksack

a beach bag

a handbag

a sports bag

a b c d e f g h i j k l m n o p q r s t u v w x y z

11

A
B
C
D
E
F
G
H
I
J
K
L
M
N
O
P
Q
R
S
T
U
V
W
X
Y
Z

ball noun

*She threw the **ball** into the air.*

a sphere
a globe

ban verb

*Our school has **banned** mobile phones.*

Use **forbid** when a person tells someone not to do something: *The teacher has **forbidden** us to talk.*

Use **prohibit** when something is not allowed because of a rule or law: *Smoking in public places is now **prohibited**.*

band noun

*I play the drums in the school **band**.*

A **group** is any band, especially one that plays pop music.

A **brass band** is a group playing trumpets and other brass instruments.

An **orchestra** is a large group of musicians playing classical music.

bang noun

*We heard a loud **bang** outside.*

a crash
a thud
a thump
a boom
an explosion

bang verb

1 *He **banged** on the door with his fists.*

To **rap** or **tap** means to bang lightly: *She **tapped** gently on the window.*

To **hammer** means to bang loudly: *He **hammered** loudly on the door.*

2 *I fell and **banged** my head.*

to bump
to knock

to hit
to bash

bare adjective

*The baby was **bare**.*

naked
undressed
nude

base noun

1 *There were plants growing along the **base** of the wall.*

the bottom
the foot

2 *The soldiers returned to their **base**.*

a headquarters
a camp

basic adjective

*You must learn the **basic** skills before trying anything complicated.*

main
key
essential
elementary

bat noun

> **WORD WEB**
>
> *Some types of **bat**:*
> **a badminton racket**
> **a baseball bat**
> **a cricket bat**
> **a golf club**
> **a hockey stick**
> **a shinty stick**
> **a tennis racket**

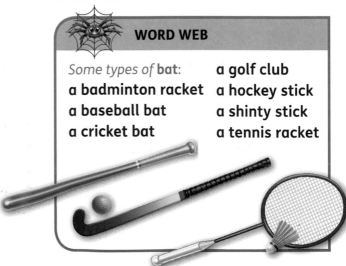

beach noun

The children played on the beach.

the sand

the seaside

the seashore

the shore

Shingle is a pebbly beach: *We walked over the shingle, looking for colourful pebbles.*

bear verb bears, bearing, bore

1 *The ice may not bear your weight.*

to support

to hold

2 *I can't bear loud music!*

to stand

to put up with

beast noun

A huge beast roamed the forest.

a creature

a monster

a brute

a wild animal

beat verb

1 *We beat the other team 1–0.*

to defeat

To **thrash** someone means to beat them very easily: *They thrashed us 6–0.*

2 *It's cruel to beat animals.*

to hit

to thrash

to whip

3 *Beat the eggs and sugar together.*

to mix

to blend

to stir

to whip

beautiful adjective

> **OVERUSED WORD**
>
> Here are some more interesting words for **beautiful**:
>
> **1** *He married the beautiful princess.*
>
> **lovely**
>
> **pretty**
>
> **fair**
>
> **attractive**
>
> Use **gorgeous** or **stunning** if someone is very beautiful: *You look absolutely stunning in that dress!*
>
> Use **glamorous** if someone looks beautiful and rich: *She looked like a glamorous actress.*
>
> OPPOSITE **ugly**
>
> **2** *The weather was beautiful for sports day.*
>
> **lovely**
>
> **gorgeous**
>
> **wonderful**
>
> **fantastic**
>
> **fine**
>
> OPPOSITE **awful**

became verb past tense see become

become verb becomes, becoming, became

1 *A tadpole will become a frog.*

to change into

to grow into

to turn into

2 *He became angry.*

to get

to grow

a
b
c
d
e
f
g
h
i
j
k
l
m
n
o
p
q
r
s
t
u
v
w
x
y
z

13

bed noun

WORD WEB

Some types of **bed**:

a berth a bed on a ship

a bunk one of two beds on top of each other

a cot a bed with sides for a baby

a four-poster bed a bed with curtains around it

a hammock a piece of cloth that you hang up and use as a bed

beg verb

We **begged** *him to let us go.*

to ask

to plead with *We* **pleaded with** *him to let us go.*

to implore *We* **implored** *him to let us go.*

began verb past tense see begin

begin verb begins, beginning, began

1 *The little girl* **began** *to laugh.*

to start

2 *At what time does the concert* **begin**?

to start

to commence

OPPOSITE end

beginning noun

I was scared at the **beginning** *of the story and hid under the covers.*

the start

the opening

OPPOSITE ending

behave verb

1 *She was* **behaving** *rather strangely.*

to act

2 *Make sure you* **behave** *at the party.*

to be good

to behave yourself

to be on your best behaviour

belief noun

People have different religious **beliefs**.

a faith

an opinion

a view

believe verb

1 *I don't* **believe** *what you are saying to me.*

to trust

2 *I* **believe** *that she is innocent.*

to think

to be sure

to be convinced

3 *The ancient Greeks* **believed** *in many gods.*

to have faith in

to put your faith in

bell noun

WRITING TIPS

Here are some useful words for writing about **bells**:

• *The school bell* **rings** *at ten to nine.*

• *The grandfather clock in the hall* **chimes** *every hour.*

• *The sleigh bells* **jingled** *as we rode along in the snow.*

• *The tiny bells on the Christmas tree* **tinkled** *as I walked past.*

• *The huge church bell began to* **toll**.

belong verb
1 *This MP3 player* **belongs** *to me.*
to be owned by
2 *Ben* **belongs** *to the running club.*
to be a member of
to be in *Ben* **is in** *the football club.*
3 *These pencils* **belong** *in the cupboard.*
to go

belongings noun
Be sure to take your **belongings** *when you get off the train.*
possessions
property
things

bend noun
There are a lot of sharp **bends** *in this road.*
a corner
a turn
a twist
a curve

bend verb
1 *He* **bent** *the wire into the correct shape.*
to twist
to curve
to curl
to coil
to wind
OPPOSITE **straighten**
2 *She* **bent** *down to tie her shoelaces.*
to stoop
to crouch
to duck

bent adjective
The back wheel of the bicycle was **bent**.
twisted
crooked
distorted
OPPOSITE **straight**

best adjective
She is the **best** *swimmer in the world.*
finest
greatest
number-one
top
OPPOSITE **worst**

better adjective
Tom has been ill, but he's **better** *now.*
all right
recovered
cured

beware verb
Beware of the dog.
to be careful of
to watch out for

a
b
c
d
e
f
g
h
i
j
k
l
m
n
o
p
q
r
s
t
u
v
w
x
y
z

A B C D E F G H I J K L M N O P Q R S T U V W X Y Z

bicycle noun
a bike
a cycle

WORD WEB

Some types of **bicycle:**
- **a hybrid bike** a cross between a road bike and a mountain bike
- **a mountain bike**
- **a racing bike**
- **a tandem** for two people
- **a tricycle** with three wheels
- **a unicycle** with one wheel

a mountain bike

a unicycle

a tandem

big adjective

OVERUSED WORD

Here are some more interesting words for **big**:

1 *He put the books into a **big** box.*

Use **large** when you want to say that something is quite big: *There was a **large** wooden crate in the middle of the room.*

Use **huge** or **enormous** for something that is very big: *We had to climb over some **huge** rocks.*

Use **massive**, **gigantic**, or **colossal** for something that is very big indeed: *The dragon swept the ship aside with one of its **colossal** claws.*

2 *There are lots of **big** buildings in the city centre.*

large
tall
high

Use **spacious** for houses and flats that have plenty of space inside: *Inside, the flat was quite **spacious**.*

Use **vast** for very big buildings, ships, or rooms: *Underneath the house was a **vast** cellar.*

Use **grand** or **magnificent** for things that are big and beautiful: *We were amazed by the **magnificent** mountains.*

3 *Tom is quite **big** for his age.*

tall

Use **broad** or **well-built** for someone who looks strong and not very thin: *He was a strong, **well-built** boy.*

4 *This T-shirt is too **big** for me.*

long
loose
baggy

5 *Mice are a **big** problem for farmers.*

important
serious
significant
OPPOSITE **small**

bird noun

WORD WEB

Some familiar British birds:
blackbird
blue tit
chaffinch
crow
cuckoo
dove
house martin
lark
magpie
pigeon
robin
sparrow
starling
swallow
thrush
woodpecker
wren

Some birds of prey:
buzzard
eagle
falcon
hawk
kestrel
kite
owl
peregrine falcon
vulture

Some farm birds:
chicken
duck
goose
turkey

Some water birds:
coot
curlew
duck
flamingo
heron
kingfisher
moorhen
pelican
swan

Some seabirds:
albatross
penguin
puffin
seagull

Some tropical birds:
budgerigar
canary
cockatoo
macaw
magpie
mynah bird
parakeet
parrot
toucan

a macaw

a duck

a puffin

a kestrel

a blue tit

a kingfisher

WRITING TIPS

Here are some useful words for writing about **birds**. Some describe movement, and others sound. Next time you see or hear a bird, think about which words you would use to describe it.

• *A strange-looking bird* **flew** *past me.*
• *The eagle* **soared** *high in the sky.*
• *I watched the large bird* **hover** *and* **glide**, *then* **swoop** *down on its prey.*
• *Sparrows* **fluttered** *about in the trees.*
• *A robin* **hopped** *onto the branch next to me.*
• *I could hear birds* **singing** *early in the morning.*
• *The little birds* **twittered** *and* **chirped** *in trees.*
• *Owls* **screeched** *and* **hooted** *in the wood.*

Then one day, a truly magnificent bird flew down out of the sky and landed on the monkey cage.—Roald Dahl, *The Twits*

bit noun

OVERUSED WORD

Here are some more interesting words for **bit**:

Use **piece** with exactly the same meaning as bit: *I've lost a* **piece** *of my jigsaw.*

Use **chunk**, **lump**, **block**, or **slab** for a big bit of something: *It was a big* **lump** *of rock.*

Use **fragment** for a small bit of something: *We found some tiny* **fragments** *of Roman pottery.*

Use **slice** or **sliver** for a thin bit of something: *Would you like a* **slice** *of cake?*

Use **scrap** for a small bit of paper or cloth: *I wrote the address down on a* **scrap** *of paper.*

Use **chip** for a small bit that has broken off something: *He found a* **chip** *of glass on the floor.*

Use **bite, mouthful, nibble,** or **taste** for a small bit of something you eat: *Can I have a* **bite** *of your biscuit?*

bite verb bites, biting, bit

1 *Be careful that horse doesn't* **bite** *you.*
to nip
to snap at
2 *The mice* **bit** *a hole in the carpet!*
to chew
to gnaw
to nibble

bitter adjective

The medicine had a **bitter** *taste.*
sour
sharp
acid
OPPOSITE **sweet**

black adjective

1 *It was a cold,* **black** *night.*
dark
pitch black
moonless
2 *She had* **black** *hair.*
dark
jet black
ebony

blame verb
*The teacher **blamed** me for breaking the window.*

to accuse *The teacher **accused** me of breaking the window.*

to tell off *The teacher **told me off** for breaking the window.*

to scold *The teacher **scolded** me for breaking the window.*

blew verb past tense *see* blow

blob noun
*There was a **blob** of jam on the table.*

a lump
a dollop
a drop

block noun
*They covered the hole with a **block** of concrete.*

a piece
a lump
a slab

block verb
*A huge lorry had **blocked** the road.*

to obstruct
to clog up

blow verb blows, blowing, blew
*He **blew** on his food to cool it down.*

to breathe
to puff

blue adjective
navy blue
sky-blue
royal blue
turquoise

blush verb
*She **blushed** a bright red whenever a boy spoke to her.*

to go red
to redden
to flush

boast verb
*She's always **boasting** about how good she is at netball.*

to brag
to show off
to gloat

boat noun
*We need a **boat** to get across the lake.*

a ship
a vessel
a craft

WORD WEB

*Some types of **boat**:*

an aircraft carrier
a barge
a battleship
a canoe
a dinghy
a ferry
a fishing boat
a kayak
a lifeboat
a motorboat
a raft
a rowing boat
a sailing boat
a speedboat
a tanker
a trawler
a warship
a yacht

A B C D E F G H I J K L M N O P Q R S T U V W X Y Z

WRITING TIPS

Here are some useful words for writing about **boats**:

- The little fishing boat **bobbed up and down** in the water.
- The dinghy **drifted** slowly out to sea.
- We **floated** down the river on our raft.
- The barge **chugged** slowly along the canal.
- The speedboat **sped** quickly through the water.

- We **sailed** the yacht into the harbour and **moored** it to the jetty.
- We were worried our little rowing boat would **capsize** in the storm.

He leant back in his seat and surveyed the cushions, the oars, the rowlocks, and all the fascinating fittings, and felt the boat sway lightly under him.— Kenneth Grahame, *The Wind in the Willows*

body noun

WORD WEB

Some parts of your **body**:

ankle	skin
armpit	stomach
calf	thigh
cheek	throat
chest	thumb
chin	toe
ear	waist
elbow	wrist
eye	
finger	
forehead	
heel	
hip	
knee	
lip	
mouth	
navel	
neck	
nose	
shin	
shoulder	

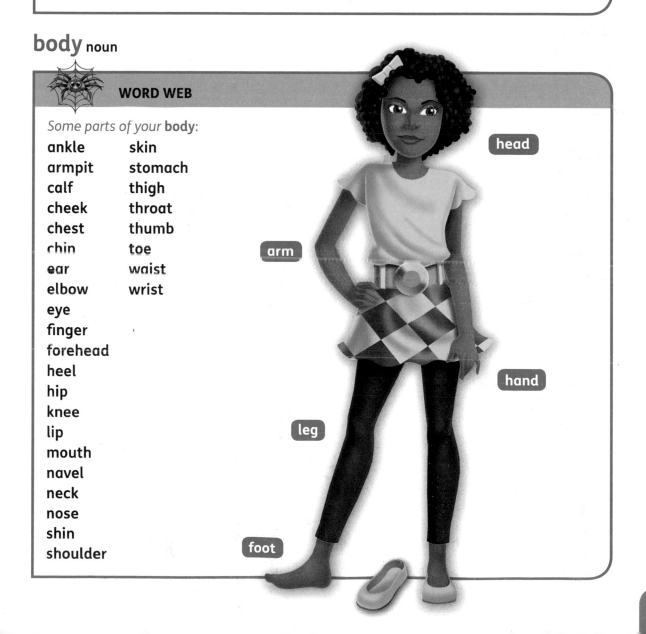

head

arm

hand

leg

foot

A
B
C
D
E
F
G
H
I
J
K
L
M
N
O
P
Q
R
S
T
U
V
W
X
Y
Z

bog noun

*You don't want to sink into the **bog** so try and walk around it.*

a marsh

a swamp

boil verb

*I'll **boil** some water to make a cup of tea.*

to bubble

to simmer

bolt verb

1 *He **bolts** the door when he goes to bed at night.*

to lock

to fasten

2 *The horse **bolted** from the stable.*

to run away

to flee

3 *She **bolted** her food as she was so hungry.*

to gobble down

to guzzle

to wolf

book noun

WORD WEB

*Some types of **book**:*
an annual	**a non-fiction book**
an atlas	**a novel**
a brochure	**a picture book**
a catalogue	**a reference book**
a comic	**a story book**
a dictionary	**a textbook**
a directory	**a thesaurus**
an encyclopedia	
an e-book	

bore verb past tense *see* bear

boring adjective

*This book is really **boring**!*

dull

tedious

dreary

Use **uneventful** or **unexciting** when nothing interesting happens: *It was a very **uneventful** day.*

Use **monotonous** to describe a boring voice: *The doctor spoke in a low, **monotonous** voice.*
OPPOSITE **interesting**

borrow verb

*Can I **borrow** your pen for a minute, please?*

to use

to take

boss noun

1 *Who's the **boss** here?*

the person in charge

the leader

the chief

the head

2 *Her **boss** said she could have the day off.*

an employer

a manager

a supervisor

a director

bossy adjective

*She can be **bossy** sometimes.*

domineering

bullying

bother verb

1 *Is the loud music **bothering** you?*

to annoy

to disturb
to upset
to irritate
2 *They didn't **bother** to clear up their mess.*
to make the effort
to take the trouble

bottom noun

1 *We'll wait at the **bottom** of the hill.*
the foot
the base
OPPOSITE **top**
2 *She fell and landed on her **bottom**.*
backside
rear

bought verb past tense *see* buy

bowl noun

*She put the fruit into a **bowl**.*
a dish
a basin

box noun

1 *I bought a **box** of cereal.*
a packet
a carton
2 *We packed the books into a **box**.*
a case
a crate
a chest
a trunk

brave adjective

*Are you **brave** enough to fight the dragon?*
courageous
bold
daring

Use **fearless** if someone seems to feel no fear: *The captain was **fearless** in battle.*

Use **heroic** if someone helps another person in a very brave way: *The firemen were rewarded for their **heroic** rescue of the boy.*

Use **adventurous** if someone is brave enough to start a new adventure: *Are you **adventurous** enough to do this challenge?*
OPPOSITE **cowardly**

bravery noun

*He got a medal for his **bravery**.*
courage
heroism
valour
OPPOSITE **cowardice**

break verb breaks, breaking, broke

1 *I dropped a cup and it **broke**.*
to crack
Use **chip** when a small piece breaks off something: *I **chipped** my favourite mug.*
Use **smash**, **shatter**, and **splinter** when something breaks into a lot of pieces: *The glass **shattered** into hundreds of tiny pieces*
2 *The stick **broke** into two pieces.*
to snap
to split
3 *The bridge will **break** if there is too much weight on it.*
to collapse
to fall down
to fall apart
4 *My brother **broke** my CD player.*
to damage
to ruin
5 *She fell and **broke** her wrist.*
to fracture
6 *You will be punished if you **break** the rules.*
to disobey

a
b
c
d
e
f
g
h
i
j
k
l
m
n
o
p
q
r
s
t
u
v
w
x
y
z

break noun

1 *We climbed through a* **break** *in the hedge.*

a gap

a hole

an opening

2 *There was a* **break** *in the oil pipe.*

a crack

a split

a hole

3 *Let's stop for a short* **break***.*

a rest

a pause

4 *There will be a fifteen-minute* **break** *halfway through the show.*

an interval

an intermission

bridge noun

WORD WEB

Some types of **bridge***:*

a flyover over a motorway

a footbridge for people

a railway bridge over a rail track

a viaduct over a river or valley

bright adjective

1 *We saw a* **bright** *light in the sky as the aeroplane flew over.*

shining

gleaming

Use **dazzling** and **brilliant** for a light that is very bright: *We watched the* **dazzling** *firework display.*

Use **glaring** and **blinding** for a light that is so bright you cannot look at it: *We turned away from the* **blinding** *headlights.*

Use **glowing** and **gleaming** for a soft, gentle light: *We could see the* **glowing** *light of the fire in the distance.*

OPPOSITE **dull**

2 *I like wearing* **bright** *colours.*

strong

rich

vivid

OPPOSITE **dull**

3 *He's a very* **bright** *boy who is good at English, music, and maths.*

clever

intelligent

brainy *(informal)*

quick

sharp

smart

OPPOSITE **stupid**

4 *It was a lovely* **bright** *day.*

clear

fine

sunny

Use **brilliant** for a very bright day: *The next morning was a* **brilliant** *day of blue skies and hot sun.*

OPPOSITE **gloomy**

brilliant adjective

1 *She is a brilliant scientist.*

intelligent

clever

talented

OPPOSITE **stupid**

2 *It's a brilliant movie.*

great

excellent

wonderful

fantastic

marvellous

OPPOSITE **terrible**

bring verb bring, bringing, brought

1 *I'll bring the shopping in.*

to carry

to take

2 *Please bring me a drink.*

to get

to fetch

broad adjective

The stream is quite broad here.

wide

big

large

OPPOSITE **narrow**

broke verb past tense *see* break

brought verb past tense *see* bring

brown adjective

He was wearing brown trousers.

beige

fawn

khaki

chocolate brown

brush verb

We had to brush the floor.

to sweep

to clean

bug noun

1 *You can find lots of interesting bugs in your garden.*

an insect

a creepy-crawly (informal)

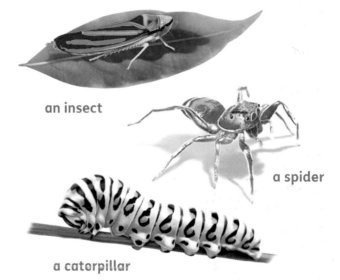

an insect

a spider

a caterpillar

2 *She has been off school with a bug.*

a virus

a germ

an illness

3 *The computer program had a bug in it.*

a fault

an error

a virus

build verb builds, building, built

It can take about six months to build a new house.

to construct

to put up

A
B
C
D
E
F
G
H
I
J
K
L
M
N
O
P
Q
R
S
T
U
V
W
X
Y
Z

building noun

WORD WEB

Some **buildings** *where people live:*

an apartment
a bungalow
a castle
a cottage
a farmhouse
a flat
a house
a mansion
a palace
a skyscraper
a tower
a villa

Other types of building:

a cafe
a cinema
a doctor's surgery
a factory
a fire station
a garage
a hospital
a hotel
a library
a mill
a museum
an office

a police station
a post office
a prison
a school
a shop
a theatre

Some **buildings** *where people worship:*

a cathedral
a chapel
a church
a gurdwara

a monastery
a mosque
a synagogue
a temple

---

built verb past tense *see* build

bully verb

Some of the older boys were **bullying** *him.*

to tease
to torment

Use **terrorize** and **persecute** when someone bullies a person badly: *He used to* **terrorize** *the younger children and take all their money off them.*

bump noun

1 *The book fell to the ground with a huge* **bump**.

a bang
a crash
a thud
a thump

2 *She's got a nasty* **bump** *on her head.*

a lump
a swelling

bump verb

I fell and **bumped** *my head.*

to bang
to knock
to hit
to bash

bumpy adjective

We drove along the **bumpy** *road.*

rough
uneven

bunch noun

1 *He bought me a* **bunch** *of flowers.*

a bouquet
a posy

2 *She handed me a large **bunch** of keys.*
a collection
a set
a quantity
3 *I went to the park with a **bunch** of friends.*
a group
a crowd
a gang

burn verb

1 *Paper **burns** easily.*
to catch fire
to catch light
to burst into flames
2 *A fire was **burning** in the grate.*
Use **blaze** when a fire burns quickly, with a lot of heat: *A warm fire **blazed** in the corner.*
Use **glow** or **smoulder** when a fire burns slowly, without big flames: *Last night's bonfire was still **smouldering** in the garden.*
Use **flicker** when a fire burns with small flames: *The camp fire **flickered** merrily.*
3 *We can **burn** all this rubbish.*
to set fire to
to set alight
to incinerate
4 *He **burned** his shirt on the iron.*
to scorch
to singe

burst verb bursts, bursting, burst

*My balloon's **burst**!*
to pop
to go bang
to split

bus noun

a coach
a minibus

business noun

1 *His parents run their own **business**.*
a company
a firm
an organization
2 *Her dad works in **business**.*
commerce
industry
trade

busy adjective

1 *Dad was **busy** in the garden.*
occupied
working
OPPOSITE **idle**
2 *I've had a very **busy** morning.*
active
energetic
OPPOSITE **idle**
3 *London is a very **busy** place.*
crowded
bustling
lively
OPPOSITE **peaceful**

buy verb buys, buying, bought

1 *Where's the best place to **buy** a mountain bike?*
to get
to purchase
to obtain
2 *My friend **bought** me some grapes when I was in hospital.*
to get *My friend **got** me some grapes.*
to treat someone to *My friend **treated me to** some grapes.*
to pay for *My friend **paid for** some grapes for me.*
OPPOSITE **sell**

a b c d e f g h i j k l m n o p q r s t u v w x y z

27

A
B
C
D
E
F
G
H
I
J
K
L
M
N
O
P
Q
R
S
T
U
V
W
X
Y
Z

Cc

cafe noun

We went to a cafe for lunch.

a **restaurant**
a **snack bar**
a **coffee bar**
a **tea room**
a **cafeteria**

cage noun

WORD WEB

Some types of cage:
an aviary for birds
an enclosure in a zoo
a hutch for rabbits
a pen for farm animals

call verb

1 *'Hello,' she called.*

to **shout**
to **yell**
to **cry**

2 *We've decided to call the puppy Lucky.*

to **name**

3 *I'll call you when I get home.*

to **phone**
to **ring**
to **telephone**

calm adjective

1 *The little village was very calm.*

peaceful
quiet
OPPOSITE **noisy**

2 *The sea was calm after the storm.*

flat
smooth
still
OPPOSITE **stormy**

3 *It was a lovely calm day, and not a leaf moved on the trees.*

still
windless
OPPOSITE **windy**

4 *She asked the children to keep calm.*

quiet
relaxed
cool
patient
OPPOSITE **excited**

came verb past tense *see* come

car noun

WRITING TIPS

Here are some useful words for writing about **cars**:

• *The little car **accelerated** down the hill then **slowed** down and **stopped** at the traffic lights.*

• *The sports car was **speeding** along.*

• *Cars **zoomed** past us on the road.*

• *The taxi **raced** away towards the airport.*

• *The old estate car **crawled along** at 40 kilometres per hour.*

'Your sons flew that car to Harry's house and back last night,' shouted Mrs Weasley. 'What have you got to say about that, eh?' 'Did you really?' said Mr Weasley eagerly. —J. K. Rowling, *Harry Potter and the Chamber of Secrets*

WORD WEB

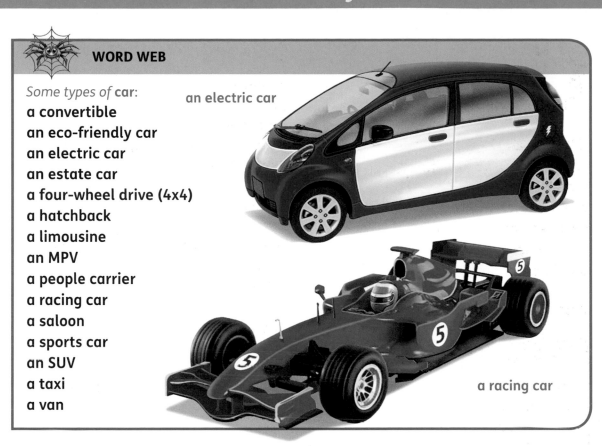

Some types of **car:**
a convertible
an eco-friendly car
an electric car
an estate car
a four-wheel drive (4x4)
a hatchback
a limousine
an MPV
a people carrier
a racing car
a saloon
a sports car
an SUV
a taxi
a van

an electric car

a racing car

care verb

I don't **care** *who wins the game.*
to mind *I don't* **mind** *who wins.*
to be bothered *I'm not* **bothered** *who wins.*

careful adjective

1 *Be* **careful** *when you cross the busy road.*
cautious
alert
attentive
watchful
2 *This is good,* **careful** *work.*
neat
thorough
conscientious
accurate
OPPOSITE **careless**

careless adjective

1 *This work is untidy and* **careless**!
messy
untidy
sloppy *(informal)*
shoddy
2 *She was* **careless** *and left the door open.*
silly
foolish
thoughtless
irresponsible
OPPOSITE **careful**

carry verb

We **carried** *the boxes into the house.*
to lift
to move
to bring
to take

carry on

*The children **carried on** talking after they had been told to be quiet.*

to continue

to keep on

to go on

case noun

1 *We packed the books into wooden **cases**.*

a box

a crate

a container

2 *He left his **case** on the train.*

a suitcase

a bag

castle noun

a fort

a fortress

a stronghold

cat noun

*A large black **cat** was sitting on the wall.*

a pussy

a pussy cat

a moggy *(informal)*

*A **kitten** is a young cat, a **tomcat** is a male cat.*

WORD WEB

*Some types of wild **cat**:*

a cheetah

a leopard

a lion

a lynx

an ocelot

a panther

a puma

a tiger

a wildcat

*Some types of domestic **cat**:*

a Manx cat

a Persian cat

a Siamese cat

a tabby cat

a tortoiseshell cat

WRITING TIPS

Here are some useful words for writing about **cats**:

• *Cats can **creep** or **slink** along very quietly.*

• *They **prowl** around when they are looking for food, then they **crouch down** and **spring** on their prey.*

• *Cats **miaow** or **mew** when they are hungry.*

• *They **purr** when they are happy, and they **hiss** and **spit** when they are angry.*

'Well! I've often seen a cat without a grin', thought Alice; 'but a grin without a cat! It's the most curious thing I ever saw in all my life!'—Lewis Carroll, Alice's Adventures in Wonderland

A B C D E F G H I J K L M N O P Q R S T U V W X Y Z

catch verb catches, catching, caught

1 *The police have* **caught** *the thieves.*

to capture

to arrest

to take prisoner *The police have* **taken** *the thieves* **prisoner***.*

2 *We* **caught** *mice in the house and released them into the garden.*

to trap

to snare

3 *I've* **caught** *a fish!*

to hook

to net

4 *Try to* **catch** *the ball.*

to get hold of

to take hold of

to hold

to grip

to grab

5 *She* **caught** *chickenpox.*

to get

to come down with

to be infected with

caught verb past tense *see* **catch**

cause verb

The heavy rain **caused** *a lot of flooding.*

to bring about

to lead to

to result in

to produce

celebration noun

There was a huge **celebration** *when the new king was crowned.*

a party

a feast

a carnival

centre noun

1 *There was a fire in the* **centre** *of the room that kept the whole house warm.*

the middle

2 *They live right in the* **centre** *of the city.*

the middle

the heart

3 *The* **centre** *of the planet is very hot.*

the core

the middle

chair noun

He sat in his usual **chair** *by the fire and made himself comfortable.*

a seat

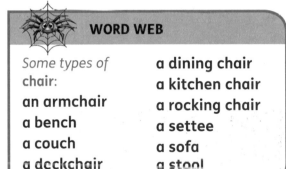

WORD WEB

Some types of chair:

an armchair
a bench
a couch
a deckchair
a dining chair
a kitchen chair
a rocking chair
a settee
a sofa
a stool

champion noun

I want to win the competition and become the world **champion***.*

the winner

the best

the victor

chance noun

1 *This is our last* **chance** *to escape.*

an opportunity

2 *There is a* **chance** *that we will fail.*

a possibility

a risk

a
b
c
d
e
f
g
h
i
j
k
l
m
n
o
p
q
r
s
t
u
v
w
x
y
z

A
B
C
D
E
F
G
H
I
J
K
L
M
N
O
P
Q
R
S
T
U
V
W
X
Y
Z

3 *We met by* **chance.**
luck
coincidence
fate

change noun
1 *We need* **change** *for the parking machine.*
coins
2 *At the weekend there will be a* **change** *in the weather.*
an alteration

change verb
1 *Our school has* **changed** *a lot in the last five years.*
to alter
2 *I* **changed** *my design because it didn't work.*
to alter
to modify
to adjust
3 *Tadpoles* **change** *into frogs.*
to turn into
to grow into
to develop into
to become
4 *I took the dress back to the shop and* **changed** *it.*
to exchange
to swap

character noun
1 *Which* **character** *would you like to be in the school play?*
a part
a role
2 *Tom has got a lovely* **character.**
a personality
a nature
a temperament

charge noun
There is no **charge** *to go into the exhibition at the museum.*
a fee
a payment

charge verb
1 *How much do they* **charge** *for orange juice?*
to ask
2 *The bull was about to* **charge.**
to attack
to rush
to stampede

charming adjective
What a **charming** *little dog!*
lovely
pretty
beautiful
delightful
cute *(informal)*

chart noun
We drew a **chart** *to show the results of the school's sponsored swim.*
a graph
a diagram
a table

chase verb
1 *The policeman* **chased** *the thief down the road.*
to run after
to follow
to pursue
2 *It is natural for* **cats** *to chase birds.*
to hunt
to track
to catch

chat verb

*Stop **chatting** to each other and get on with your work!*

to talk
to chatter
to natter

To **gossip** means to talk about other people: *I thought all the other girls were **gossiping** about me.*

cheat verb

1 *The other team won, but we all thought they **cheated**!*

to break the rules
to not play fair

2 *They **cheated** me out of my money.*

to trick
to swindle
to fool

check verb

1 *Always **check** your spellings.*

to look at
to examine
to double-check

2 *All the cars are carefully **checked** before they are sold.*

to inspect
to test

cheeky adjective

*Don't be so **cheeky** to you parents!*

rude
impertinent
impudent
insolent
disrespectful
OPPOSITE **respectful**

cheer verb

*Everyone **cheered** when our team scored.*

to shout
to applaud

cheerful adjective

*He seems very **cheerful** today.*

happy
smiling
joyful
light-hearted
OPPOSITE **sad**

chew verb

1 *She was **chewing** on an apple.*

Use **to bite** when you sink your teeth into something: *I **bit** into the warm pie.*

Use **to crunch** when something is crispy or hard: *Ben **crunched** the crispy apple.*

Use **to suck** when something is too soft to bite into: *Samir **sucked** the ice lolly.*

Use **to munch** when someone is really enjoying what they are eating: *Alice **munched** on her peanut butter sandwich.*

Use **to nibble** when someone is eating something with small bites: *The rabbit **nibbled** on the lettuce.*

2 *Mice had **chewed** through the wires.*

to bite
to gnaw
to nibble

child noun

a boy
a girl
a kid
a youngster

A **toddler** is a young child who is just starting to walk.

a b **c** d e f g h i j k l m n o p q r s t u v w x y z

33

A
B
C
D
E
F
G
H
I
J
K
L
M
N
O
P
Q
R
S
T
U
V
W
X
Y
Z

childish adjective

*This behaviour is very **childish**!*

silly
immature
juvenile
babyish
OPPOSITE **mature**

chilly adjective

*It's a **chilly** evening so wear a jacket.*

cold
cool
nippy
fresh
frosty
OPPOSITE **warm**

choice noun

1 *You can have first **choice**.*

pick

2 *There's a **choice** of vanilla, strawberry, and chocolate ice cream.*

a selection

choke verb

1 *The thick smoke was **choking** us.*

to suffocate
to asphyxiate

2 *The tight collar was **choking** him.*

to strangle
to throttle

choose verb chooses, choosing, chose

1 *Which cake shall I **choose**?*

to pick
to select
to decide on

2 *We need to **choose** a new class representative.*

to elect
to vote for

chop verb

*My dad was **chopping** wood.*

to cut
to saw
to split

chose verb past tense *see* choose

claim verb

*She walked up to **claim** her prize.*

to ask for
to collect
to request
to demand

clap verb

*The audience **clapped** when the music finished.*

to applaud
to cheer

class noun

*Which **class** are you in?*

a form
a group
a set

clean adjective

1 *After two hours the whole house was **clean**.*

spotless
tidy
spick and span
OPPOSITE **dirty**

2 *The water in this river is very* **clean**.

fresh
pure
clear
unpolluted
OPPOSITE **polluted**

3 *Start again on a* **clean** *sheet of paper.*

blank
unused
new

clean verb

1 *They had to stay and* **clean** *the floors.*

to brush
to sweep
to hoover
to vacuum
to wash
to mop
to scrub

2 *Whose job is it to* **clean** *the windows?*

to dust
to wipe
to polish

3 *Go and* **clean** *your hands.*

to wash
to scrub
to rinse

4 *Don't forget to* **clean** *your teeth.*

to brush

clear adjective

1 *Make sure you write nice* **clear** *instructions.*

simple
plain
understandable

2 *Her voice was loud and* **clear**.

audible
distinct
understandable

3 *It was* **clear** *that he was very angry.*

obvious
evident

4 *Windows are usually made of* **clear** *glass.*

see-through
transparent
OPPOSITE **opaque**

5 *The water in the lake was lovely and* **clear**.

clean
pure
OPPOSITE **dirty**

6 *The next morning the sky was* **clear**.

blue
sunny
cloudless
OPPOSITE **cloudy**

clear verb

We need to **clear** *these chairs out of the way.*

to move
to remove
to take away

clever adjective

1 *You're so* **clever**!

intelligent
bright
brainy *(informal)*
quick
sharp
smart

2 *That's a very* **clever** *idea.*

good
brilliant
sensible
ingenious

3 *The old fox was very* **clever**.

cunning
crafty
OPPOSITE **stupid**

a
b
c
d
e
f
g
h
i
j
k
l
m
n
o
p
q
r
s
t
u
v
w
x
y
z

climb verb

1 *He climbed up the stairs.*
to go up
to run up
2 *The plane climbed into the air.*
to rise
to ascend
to go up
3 *They climbed over the rocks.*
to clamber
to scramble

clock noun

WORD WEB

Some types of clock:
an alarm clock
a cuckoo clock
a digital clock
a grandfather clock
a grandmother clock
a wind-up clock

close adjective

1 *He sat close to the fire.*
near to
next to
beside
OPPOSITE **far away**
2 *I took a close look at the map.*
careful
detailed

close verb

Please close the door.
to shut
to lock
Use **slam** when someone closes a door very noisily: *She slammed the door angrily.*
OPPOSITE **open**

clothes noun

He was dressed in old-fashioned clothes.
clothing
attire

WORD WEB

Some informal clothes:
jeans
a polo shirt
a sweatshirt
a t-shirt
a tracksuit

Some clothes for warm weather:
a blouse
a dress
a shirt
shorts
a skirt
a sunhat
trousers

Some smart clothes:

a blazer
an evening gown
a jacket
a suit
a tie
a uniform
a waistcoat

*Some **clothes** for cold weather:*

an anorak	**a duffel coat**	**a parka**	**a djellaba**
a beanie hat	**a fleece**	**a pullover**	**a kimono**
a cardigan	**gloves**	**a raincoat**	**a salwar kameez**
a cloak	**a jumper**	**a scarf**	**a sari**
a coat	**mittens**	**a sweater**	**a sarong**
		a woolly hat	**a yashmak**

*Some **clothes** from around the world:*

a b **c** d e f g h i j k l m n o p q r s t u v w x y z

37

cloudy adjective

It was a cloudy day.

grey
dull
overcast
gloomy
OPPOSITE clear

club noun

She joined her local drama club.

a society
a group
an association

clumsy adjective

I can be quite clumsy sometimes.

careless
accident-prone

coach noun

1 *We went to London on the coach and not the train.*

a bus

2 *An athletics coach trains the team.*

a trainer
an instructor

cold adjective

1 *It's quite cold outside today.*

Use **chilly**, **cool**, and **nippy** for weather that is slightly cold: *I put my sweatshirt on because it was getting a bit chilly.*

Use **freezing** or **bitter** for weather that is very cold: *It was a bitter winter's day and there was frost on the ground.*

Use **frosty**, **icy**, **snowy**, or **wintry** when there is frost, ice, or snow: *It was a lovely frosty morning.*

2 *I'm cold!*

Use **chilly** when you feel slightly cold: *I was feeling a bit chilly after my swim in the sea.*

Use **freezing** or **frozen** when you feel very cold: *After two hours in the snow, I was absolutely frozen.*

OPPOSITE hot

collapse verb

1 *Some of the old buildings collapsed in the storm.*

to fall down
to cave in

2 *The old man collapsed in the street and had to be helped up.*

to faint
to pass out
to fall down

collect verb

1 *I collect old coins as a hobby.*

to keep
to save

2 *We have collected a lot of things for our nature table.*

to accumulate
to bring together
to gather together

3 *My mum collected me from school.*

to fetch
to pick up

collection noun

He's got a huge collection of CDs but I don't know if he listens to them all.

a set
a hoard
an assortment

colour noun

*I think we should paint the room a different **colour**.*

a shade

colourful adjective

*Everyone was wearing **colourful** clothes.*

bright
multicoloured
OPPOSITE **dull**

WORD WEB

Some shades of red:	*Some shades of green:*	*Some shades of grey:*	*Some shades of black:*
crimson	**bottle green**	**charcoal grey**	**ebony**
maroon	**emerald**	**dove grey**	**jet black**
pink	**lime green**	**silver**	
purple			*Some shades of brown:*
ruby	*Some shades of yellow:*	*Some shades of white:*	**beige**
scarlet	**gold**	**cream**	**bronze**
	lemon	**ivory**	**chocolate**
Some shades of blue:	**primrose**	**snow white**	**fawn**
aquamarine			**khaki**
azure			**tan**
navy blue			
royal blue			
sapphire			
sky blue			
turquoise			

a b **c** d e f g h i j k l m n o p q r s t u v w x y z

combine verb

1 **Combine** *all the ingredients in a bowl.*

to put together
to mix together
to add together
to blend

2 *The two groups* **combined** *to make one big group.*

to come together
to join together
to unite
to merge

come verb comes, coming, came

1 *We saw a car* **coming** *towards us.*

to move
to approach *We saw a car* **approaching** *us.*
to draw near *We saw a car* **draw near** *to us.*

2 *Would you like to* **come** *to my house?*

to visit

3 *A letter* **came** *this morning.*

to arrive
to turn up

comfort verb

I **comforted** *Samir because he was upset.*

to reassure
to calm down
to cheer up

comfortable adjective

1 *This chair is very* **comfortable**.

soft
cosy
relaxing

2 *Are you* **comfortable** *on that high stool?*

relaxed
cosy

warm
happy
snug
OPPOSITE **uncomfortable**

command verb

She **commanded** *us stop loitering and to leave the classroom.*

to tell
to order
to instruct

common adjective

1 *These birds are quite* **common** *in Europe.*

widespread

2 *Earthquakes are* **common** *in this part of the world.*

frequent

3 *Having your tonsils out is a* **common** *operation.*

routine
standard

4 *It is very* **common** *for children to feel nervous before injections.*

ordinary
usual
normal
OPPOSITE **rare**

company noun

1 *I took Alice with me for* **company**.

friendship
companionship

2 *They run a* **company** *that makes apple juice.*

a business
a factory
a firm

competition noun

1 *It's a competition to see who's the best.*

a contest

a game

a race

2 *Our team won the competition.*

a tournament

a championship

complain verb

Everyone complained about the tasteless food in the canteen.

to moan

to grumble

to whinge

complete adjective

1 *I haven't got a complete set of cards.*

full

whole

entire

OPPOSITE **incomplete**

2 *At last the work was complete.*

finished

OPPOSITE **unfinished**

3 *The show was a complete disaster.*

total

absolute

utter

complicated adjective

1 *This is a very complicated machine.*

complex

sophisticated

intricate

2 *We had to do some complicated sums.*

difficult

hard

OPPOSITE **simple**

computer noun

WORD WEB

Some types of computer:

a desktop

a laptop

a notebook

a palmtop

a PC or **personal computer**

a tablet

concentrate verb

I can't concentrate with all that noise!

to think

to work

to pay attention

to focus

concerned adjective

We were all very concerned about you.

worried

anxious

confess verb

Sarah confessed that she had eaten the fruit.

to admit

to own up

to tell the truth

confident adjective

1 *She looked very calm and confident.*

self-assured

unafraid

assertive

2 *We are confident that we can win.*

sure

certain

convinced

positive

a b c d e f g h i j k l m n o p q r s t u v w x y z

A
B
C
D
E
F
G
H
I
J
K
L
M
N
O
P
Q
R
S
T
U
V
W
X
Y
Z

confuse verb

The instructions that came with the game **confused** *me.*

to puzzle
to baffle
to bewilder
to perplex

confused adjective

I was feeling very **confused** *by the instructions that came with the game.*

puzzled
bewildered
baffled

connect verb

You need to **connect** *this wire to the battery for the machine to work.*

to join
to attach
to fix

considerate adjective

Please try to be more **considerate** *of other people.*

thoughtful
kind
helpful
unselfish
OPPOSITE **selfish**

constant adjective

I'm fed up with the **constant** *noise coming from the next room.*

incessant
continuous
relentless
never-ending

construct verb

We **constructed** *a model aeroplane.*

to build
to make
to assemble

contain verb

The bag **contained** *some gold coins.*

to hold
to have inside

contest noun

We're having a jumping **contest**.

a competition
a match
a championship

continue verb

1 Continue *reading until the end of the chapter.*

to go on
to keep on
to carry on

2 *The rain* **continued** *all afternoon.*

to last
to go on
to carry on

contribute verb

1 *They* **contributed** *money to the school repair fund.*

to give
to donate
to make a donation *They* **made a donation** *to the school repair fund.*

2 *He* **contributed** *ideas to the class discussion.*

to add
to put forward

control verb

*The pilot uses these levers to **control** the aeroplane.*

to guide
to move
to direct

conversation noun

*We had a long **conversation** about sport.*

a talk
a discussion
a chat

cook verb

WORD WEB

Some ways to **cook** *meat:*
to barbecue
to casserole
to fry
to grill
to roast
to stew

Some ways to **cook** *eggs:*
to boil
to fry
to poach
to scramble

Some ways to **cook** *bread or cakes:*
to bake
to toast

Some ways to **cook** *vegetables:*
to bake
to boil
to fry
to roast
to simmer
to steam
to stir-fry

stir-fry

cool adjective

1 *It's quite **cool** outside today.*
cold
chilly
nippy
2 *I could do with a nice, **cool** drink.*
cold
ice-cold
OPPOSITE **hot**

copy verb

1 *See if you can **copy** this picture.*
to reproduce
to make a copy of
2 *Sam can **copy** his teacher's voice.*
to imitate
to mimic
to impersonate

corner noun

*I'll meet you on the **corner**, by the school.*
a crossroads
a turning
a junction
a bend

correct adjective

1 *That is the **correct** answer.*
right
2 *Make sure all your sums are **correct**.*
accurate
exact
right
OPPOSITE **wrong**

correct verb

*Shall I **correct** my mistakes?*
to put right
to rectify

A
B
C
D
E
F
G
H
I
J
K
L
M
N
O
P
Q
R
S
T
U
V
W
X
Y
Z

costume noun
*We wore special **costumes** for the play.*
clothes
a disguise
fancy dress
an outfit

cosy adjective
*The room was small and **cosy**.*
comfortable
snug
warm

count verb
*Can you **count** how many blocks of chocolate there are altogether?*
to add up
to calculate
to work out

5x3=?

country noun
1 *Australia is a big **country**.*
a land
a nation
2 *Do you live in the **country** or in a town?*
the countryside

courage noun
*We were all impressed with Ben's **courage**.*
bravery
heroism
valour

cover noun
1 *Sarah put a **cover** over the dish.*
a lid
a top
a covering
2 *He laid a **cover** over the sleeping baby.*
a blanket
a duvet

cover verb
1 *Ben pulled his sleeve down to **cover** the scar on his arm.*
to hide
to conceal
2 *She **covered** him with a blanket as he slept.*
to wrap someone in *She **wrapped him in** a blanket.*

crack noun
1 *Ben handed me an old cup with a **crack** in it.*
a break
a chip
2 *There was a **crack** in the wall.*
a hole
a gap
a split

crack verb
*Watch you don't **crack** the glass.*
to break
to chip
Use **smash** or **shatter** when something cracks and breaks into lots of pieces: *The mirror **smashed** into tiny pieces.*

crafty adjective

Foxes are crafty animals.

clever
cunning
sly
sneaky
wily

crash noun

1 *The two cars had a crash on the road.*

an accident
a smash
a collision

A **pile-up** is a crash with a lot of cars: *There was a huge pile-up on the road.*

2 *The tree fell down with a loud crash.*

a bang
a thud
a clatter
a bump
a thump

crash verb

1 *The car crashed into a wall.*

to smash into
to bang into
to hit *The car hit a wall.*

2 *Two lorries crashed in the car park.*

to collide
to have an accident

3 *My computer has just crashed.*

to go down

crawl verb

We crawled through the tunnel.

to creep
to climb

To **slither** means to crawl along on your stomach, like a snake: *He slithered under the gate.*

To **wriggle** means to squeeze through a very small space: *I managed to wriggle through a gap in the hedge.*

crazy adjective

1 *Everyone thought he was just a crazy old man.*

mad *(informal)*
silly
stupid
OPPOSITE **sensible**

2 *The children went crazy when they saw the clown.*

mad
berserk

creep verb creeps, creeping, crept

1 *We crept out through the window.*

to crawl
to climb

Use **slither** when you creep along on your stomach, like a snake: *Ben slithered under the side of the tent.*

Use **wriggle** when you squeeze through a very small space: *Alice managed to wriggle through the gap in the fence.*

2 *He crept away when no one was looking.*

to sneak
to slip
to steal

To **tiptoe** means to creep quietly on your toes: *I tiptoed past the sleeping guards.*

crept verb past tense *see* creep

cried verb past tense *see* cry

crime noun

You have committed a terrible crime.

an offence
a sin

criminal noun

*These **criminals** must be caught.*

a crook
a villain
a wrongdoer
a thief
a robber
a murderer
an offender

crisp adjective

*She bit into the **crisp** toast.*

crunchy
hard
OPPOSITE soft

crooked adjective

1 *We sat down by an old, **crooked** tree.*

bent
twisted
misshapen

2 *They climbed up the **crooked** path.*

winding
twisting
bendy
OPPOSITE straight

cross adjective

*My mum was really **cross** with me.*

angry
annoyed

Use **irritated** when someone is slightly cross: *My sister wouldn't shut up, and I was beginning to get a bit **irritated** with her.*

Use **furious** or **livid** when someone is very cross: *My brother was absolutely **furious** when I broke his MP3 player.*
OPPOSITE pleased

cross verb

*Take care when you **cross** the road.*

to go across
to go over

crouch verb

*She **crouched** down to pick up a shell.*

to bend
to stoop
to squat

crowd noun

*A **crowd** of people was waiting outside the theatre.*

a group
a mass
a horde

Use **mob** and **rabble** to talk about a noisy crowd: *There was a **rabble** of boys outside the museum.*

crowded adjective

*The airport was very **crowded** on the first day of the holidays.*

busy
full
packed
swarming with people
teeming with people
OPPOSITE empty

cruel adjective

1 *The king was a **cruel** man and his subjects were terrified of him.*

wicked
heartless
cold-hearted
brutal

2 *Some say bullfighting is a **cruel** sport.*
barbaric
inhumane
OPPOSITE **kind**

crunch verb

*He **crunched** his apple noisily.*
to chew
to munch
to chomp

crush verb

*Mind you don't **crush** the flowers.*
to squash
to flatten
to damage
to break

cry verb cries, crying, cried

1 *Some of the children were **crying**.*

Use **weep** if someone is crying quietly:
*A young girl was **weeping** in the garden.*

Use **wail**, **howl**, or **sob** if someone is crying noisily, or speaking as they are crying: *'What shall I do now?' she **wailed**.*

Use **snivel** or **blubber** if someone is making a lot of noise in a way that you find annoying: *'Crying won't do any good, so stop **snivelling**!' he said.*

2 *'Look out!' she **cried**.*
to shout
to yell
to call

Use **scream** or **shriek** when someone shouts something in a loud, high voice because they are frightened or annoyed: *'Get out of here!' she **screamed** angrily.*

Use **exclaim** when someone is surprised or excited: *'How wonderful!' she **exclaimed**.*

cuddle verb

*She **cuddled** Samir when he fell and hurt his knee.*
to hug
to embrace
to hold

cunning adjective

*He thought of a **cunning** plan to escape.*
clever
crafty
ingenious
sneaky

cup noun

WORD WEB

Some types of **cup**:

beakers

a tumbler

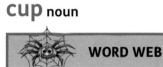
a glass

a teacup

a mug

a goblet

a b **c** d e f g h i j k l m n o p q r s t u v w x y z

A
B
C
D
E
F
G
H
I
J
K
L
M
N
O
P
Q
R
S
T
U
V
W
X
Y
Z

curious adjective

1 *We were all very* **curious** *about the new teacher.*

inquisitive

nosy

2 *There was a* **curious** *smell in the kitchen.*

strange

funny

odd

peculiar

curve noun

1 *There was a* **curve** *in the road ahead of us.*

a bend

a turn

2 *We can make a pattern using straight lines and* **curves**.

a loop

a curl

a swirl

an arc

cut noun

She had a **cut** *on her arm.*

a wound

a graze

A **nick** is a small cut: *Samir had a little* **nick** *on his finger.*

A **gash** is a big cut: *Blood was pouring from the* **gash** *on his leg.*

cut verb cuts, cutting, cut

1 *I fell over and* **cut** *my knee.*

Use **graze** or **scratch** when you do not cut yourself very badly: *I'm OK. I've just* **grazed** *my knee a bit.*

Use **wound** or **gash** when you cut yourself badly: *He* **gashed** *his leg and had to have stitches.*

2 *Cut the meat into small pieces.*

to chop

to chop up

Use **slice** when you cut something into thin pieces: *She* **sliced** *the bread and put it on a plate.*

Use **dice** when you cut something into small square pieces: **Dice** *the onion and carrot.*

Use **mince** when you cut something into tiny pieces: *For this recipe you need to* **mince** *the beef.*

3 *The hairdresser* **cut** *my hair.*

to trim

to snip

4 *The older boys* **cut** *some wood.*

to chop

to saw

to carve

Use **carve** when you cut wood into a special shape: *He* **carved** *a statue from the block of wood.*

5 *We need to* **cut** *the grass.*

to mow

6 *Dad* **cut** *the hedge.*

to prune

to trim

to clip

to cut off

cut off

He had an accident and **cut off** *one of his fingers.*

to chop off

to sever

To **amputate** someone's arm or leg means to cut it off in a special operation: *Doctors had to* **amputate** *his leg because it was so badly injured.*

Dd

damage verb

1 *Please don't bend the books in case you* **damage** *them.*

to spoil

Use **ruin** when you damage something badly: *I dropped my mobile in the bath and* **ruined** *it.*

2 *She dropped the box and* **damaged** *some of the plates.*

to break

Use **chip** when you break a little bit off something: *I* **chipped** *the paint off my new bike.*

Use **scratch** when you leave a mark on something: *You'll* **scratch** *the dining room table if you dump your school bag on it.*

Use **smash** when you break something into pieces: *I dropped the vase and* **smashed** *it.*

3 *The explosion* **damaged** *several buildings.*

to destroy

4 *The crash* **damaged** *our car quite badly.*

to dent

to wreck

5 *Someone has deliberately* **damaged** *the new fence.*

to vandalize

dance verb

1 *Everyone was* **dancing** *to the music.*

to jig about

to leap about

2 *The younger children were all* **dancing** *about with excitement.*

to skip about

to jump about

to leap about

to prance about

dance noun

He did a little **dance**.

a jig

🕷 **WORD WEB**

Some types of **dance**:

ballet
ballroom
breakdancing
country
disco
folk
Irish
line dancing
rock and roll
salsa

Scottish country dancing
tap

ballet

breakdancing

A
B
C
D
E
F
G
H
I
J
K
L
M
N
O
P
Q
R
S
T
U
V
W
X
Y
Z

danger noun

1 *The animals could sense* **danger** *from the fire in the forest.*

trouble

2 *There is a* **danger** *that you might fall.*

a risk

a chance

a possibility

dangerous adjective

1 *It's* **dangerous** *to play with matches.*

risky

unsafe

OPPOSITE **safe**

2 *A knife is a* **dangerous** *weapon.*

lethal

deadly

3 *The factory produces some very* **dangerous** *chemicals.*

harmful

poisonous

toxic

hazardous

4 *The police were searching for a* **dangerous** *criminal.*

violent

dare verb

1 *Come and catch me, if you* **dare**!

to be brave enough

to have the courage

to have the nerve

2 *I* **dare** *you to climb that tree.*

to challenge

daring adjective

Which of you boys is the most **daring**?

brave

bold

courageous

fearless

adventurous

OPPOSITE **timid**

dark adjective

1 *It was very* **dark** *outside last night.*

black

Use **pitch black** if it is completely dark: *It was* **pitch black** *in the tunnel.*

OPPOSITE **light**

2 *During the power cut the house was completely* **dark**.

Use **gloomy** or **dingy** if a room is dark and unpleasant: *The cellar was damp and* **gloomy** *and slightly spooky.*

Use **unlit** if there are no lights in the room: *We walked along a long* **unlit** *corridor.*

OPPOSITE **bright**

3 *They walked through the* **dark** *woods.*

Use **shady** if a place is nice and cool: *We found a lovely* **shady** *spot under some trees for our picnic.*

Use **shadowy** if there are lots of big shadows: *Helen hated walking through the cold,* **shadowy** *forest.*

OPPOSITE **bright**

4 *Sarah has* **dark** *hair.*

black

brown

Use **ebony** or **jet black** if someone's hair is very dark: *She had beautiful* **jet black** *hair.*

OPPOSITE **light**

dash verb

She **dashed** *out of the room when the phone rang.*

to run

to rush

to sprint

to fly
to dart
to hurry

dawdle verb

They were late for the party because they had **dawdled** *along the road.*

to stroll
to amble
to wander

dead adjective

1 *My grandmother is* **dead** *now.*

deceased
passed away *My grandmother has* **passed away**.

2 *We found the* **dead** *body of a mouse.*

lifeless

deadly adjective

Don't touch that bottle. It is poison and is **deadly**.

dangerous
lethal
fatal
OPPOSITE **harmless**

dear adjective

He was delighted to see his **dear** *daughter again.*

beloved
darling

decide verb

1 *He* **decided** *to tell his parents everything.*

to make up your mind *He* **made up his mind** *to tell his parents everything.*

to resolve *He* **resolved** *to tell his parents everything.*

2 *I can't* **decide** *which cake to have.*

to choose

decorate verb

1 *They* **decorated** *the Christmas tree with tinsel.*

to adorn
to beautify

2 *This summer we need to* **decorate** *your bedroom.*

to paint
to wallpaper

deep adjective

The treasure was hidden in a **deep** *hole.*

bottomless
OPPOSITE **shallow**

defend verb

The soldiers stayed behind to **defend** *the city.*

to protect
to guard

definite adjective

1 *The party will probably be next Saturday, but it's not* **definite** *yet.*

certain
fixed
settled

2 *I can see a* **definite** *improvement in your work.*

clear
obvious
positive

delay verb

1 *The bad weather* **delayed** *us.*

to hold someone up *The bad weather* **held us up**.

A B C D E F G H I J K L M N O P Q R S T U V W X Y Z

to make someone late *The bad weather made us late.*
2 *We had to **delay** the start of the race.*
to postpone
to put off

deliberately adverb

*Alice **deliberately** left the gate open.*

on purpose
intentionally
knowingly
OPPOSITE **accidentally**

delicious adjective

*This food is **delicious**!*

lovely

Use **tasty, scrumptious, gorgeous**, and **succulent** if food tastes delicious: *Mmm, this cake is **gorgeous**!*

Use **mouthwatering** if food looks delicious: *The table was covered with **mouthwatering** food.*
OPPOSITE **horrible**

delighted adjective

*I was **delighted** with your present.*

pleased
thrilled
overjoyed
ecstatic

deliver verb

*We will **deliver** the new computer to your house tomorrow.*

to bring
to take

demand verb

*She **demanded** an explanation for his behaviour.*

to insist on
to ask for
to request

demolish verb

*They are going to **demolish** the old school building.*

to knock down
to pull down
to bulldoze
to flatten

depend on verb

*The young chicks **depend on** their mother for food.*

to need
to rely on

describe verb

1 *She **described** the animal she had seen in the park.*

to give a description of *She **gave a description of** the animal.*

2 *Samir **described** the amazing things he'd seen on the school trip.*

to explain
to relate
to recount

design verb

*They have **designed** a new type of engine.*

to create
to make
to invent
to devise
to plan

destroy verb

1 *The hurricane **destroyed** several buildings.*
to demolish
to flatten
to crush
2 *The storm **destroyed** their small boat.*
to smash
to wreck
3 *The fire **destroyed** many old books.*
to ruin

diagram noun

*We drew a **diagram** of the machine.*
a plan
a drawing
a sketch

diary noun

*I am keeping a **diary** of our holiday.*
a journal
a daily record

did verb past tense *see* **do**

die verb

1 *My grandfather **died** last year.*
to pass away
2 *No-one **died** in the fire.*
to perish
to be killed *No-one was **killed** in the fire.*
3 *The plant **died** because I didn't water it.*
to shrivel
to wither

different adjective

1 *Your book is **different** from mine.*
dissimilar
unlike
OPPOSITE **similar**

2 *I have ten pencils in **different** colours.*
assorted
various
3 *Each one of the puppies is slightly **different**.*
special
distinctive
individual
unique
4 *Let's do something **different** for a change!*
new
exciting
unusual
extraordinary
5 *Our new neighbours are certainly **different**!*
strange
peculiar
odd
unusual
bizarre

difficult adjective

*The teacher gave us some very **difficult** work to do.*
hard
tough
tricky
complicated
OPPOSITE **easy**

dig verb digs, digging, dug

1 *We **dug** a hole in the garden.*
to make
to excavate
2 *We'll have to **dig** our way out of here!*
to tunnel
to burrow
3 *They **dig** stone out of the ground here.*
You **quarry** stone and **mine** coal: *Coal has been **mined** here for 200 years.*

a b c **d** e f g h i j k l m n o p q r s t u v w x y z

53

A
B
C
D
E
F
G
H
I
J
K
L
M
N
O
P
Q
R
S
T
U
V
W
X
Y
Z

dip verb
She dipped her hand into the water.
to lower
to drop
to plunge
to immerse

dirt noun
Their clothes were covered in dirt.
mud
muck
dust
grime
filth

dirty adjective
1 *Why are your clothes so dirty?*
Use **mucky** or **grubby** if something is slightly dirty: *His sweatshirt was old and slightly grubby.*
Use **muddy** if something is covered in mud: *Take your muddy boots off!*
Use **greasy** if something is covered in oil or grease: *He handed me a horrible greasy spoon.*
Use **filthy** or **grimy** if something is very dirty: *Go and wash your hands. They're filthy!*
Use **stained** if something has dirty marks on it: *His shirt was stained with ink.*
2 *The room was very dirty.*
dusty
messy
filthy
3 *The water in some rivers is too dirty to drink.*
polluted
foul
OPPOSITE clean

disagree verb
Sarah and Samir disagree about everything.
to argue
to quarrel
to have different opinions
OPPOSITE agree

disappear verb
The cat disappeared into the bushes.
to vanish
OPPOSITE appear

disappointed adjective
I was very disappointed when the trip was cancelled.
upset
sad
dejected
downcast

disaster noun
The warehouse fire was a terrible disaster.
a tragedy
a catastrophe
a calamity

discover verb
We discovered an old map in the attic.
to find
to come across
to uncover
to unearth

discussion noun
We had a discussion about which vegetables to plant in the garden.
a talk
a conversation
a chat

disease noun
The scientists found a cure for the **disease**.
an illness
a complaint
a sickness
an infection

disgusting adjective
This food is **disgusting** and I can't eat it!
horrible
revolting
foul
OPPOSITE lovely

dish noun
She put the vegetables in a deep **dish**.
a bowl
a plate
a platter

display noun
We made a **display** of our paintings.
an exhibition
a presentation

display verb
We will **display** the best pictures in the hall.
to show
to hang up
to exhibit

distance noun
We measured the **distance** between the two posts.
the space
the gap
the length
the width

distant adjective
They travelled to many **distant** lands.
faraway
far off
remote

disturb verb
1 I'm working, so please don't **disturb** me.
to interrupt
to bother
To **pester** or **hassle** someone means to keep disturbing them: My little brother has been **pestering** me all morning!
2 The sight of so many empty houses **disturbed** me.
to worry
to trouble
to alarm
to distress

dive verb
Ben **dived** into the water.
to plunge
to leap
to jump

divide verb
1 We can **divide** the grapes between us.
to share
to split
2 She **divided** the lasagne into ten pieces.
to cut
to split
to separate

a b c **d** e f g h i j k l m n o p q r s t u v w x y z

dizzy adjective

I felt weak and dizzy.

giddy
faint
light-headed
unsteady

do verb does, doing, did

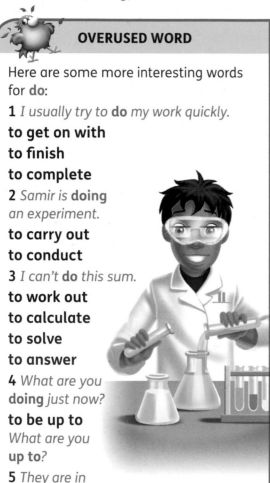

OVERUSED WORD

Here are some more interesting words for **do**:

1 *I usually try to **do** my work quickly.*

to get on with
to finish
to complete

2 *Samir is **doing** an experiment.*

to carry out
to conduct

3 *I can't **do** this sum.*

to work out
to calculate
to solve
to answer

4 *What are you **doing** just now?*

to be up to

What are you up to?

5 *They are in danger—we must **do** something!*

to take action
to act

6 *You have **done** very well.*

to get on
to perform

doctor noun

WORD WEB

Some types of **doctor**:

a consultant a doctor in a hospital

a general practitioner or **GP**

a paediatrician a doctor who looks after children

a specialist a doctor who knows a lot about one type of illness

a surgeon a doctor who performs operations

dog noun

a hound
a bitch a female dog
a puppy a young dog

WORD WEB

Some types of **dog**:

a beagle
a boxer
a bulldog
a chihuahua
a collie
a dachshund
a Dalmatian
a German Shepherd
a great Dane

a greyhound
a Labrador
a mongrel
 a mixture of different breeds
a poodle
a retriever
a sheepdog
a spaniel
a terrier

a dachshund

WRITING TIPS

Here are some useful words for writing about **dogs**:

- *The dogs **barked** and **yapped** excitedly when they heard us coming.*
- *Our dog always **whines** by the kitchen door when she wants to go out.*
- *The little dog **yelped** when I accidentally trod on his tail.*
- *The guard dog **growled** and **snarled** at us.*
- *The dog was **panting** after he had run up the hill.*

Pongo stood on his hind legs and kissed the wet dog on the nose.
—Dodie Smith, *The One Hundred and One Dalmations*

doubt noun
*There is some **doubt** about whether she will be well enough to play tennis.*

concern
worry
anxiety
uncertainty

doubt verb
*I **doubt** that I'll get to the concert on time.*

to question
to wonder
to be uncertain about

drag verb
*We **dragged** the box out into the hall.*

to pull
to haul
to tug

drank verb past tense *see* drink

draw verb draws, drawing, drew
1 *Are you good at **drawing** pictures?*

to sketch
to paint
to trace
to doodle

2 *She **drew** the curtains.*

to close
to open
to pull back

3 *The two teams **drew** in the last game.*

to finish equal
to tie

dreadful adjective
*The whole house was in a **dreadful** mess.*

terrible
awful
horrible
appalling

A
B
C
D
E
F
G
H
I
J
K
L
M
N
O
P
Q
R
S
T
U
V
W
X
Y
Z

dream noun

1 *Do you ever remember your* **dreams***?*
a bad dream a horrible dream
a nightmare a frightening dream
2 *Alice's* **dream** *is to be a vet.*
an ambition
a wish
a goal
A **fantasy** is a dream you have which you know will never come true: *Ben has this* **fantasy** *about being a pop star.*

dress noun

She was wearing a red **dress***.*
a frock
a gown

dress verb

1 *Hurry up and get* **dressed** *or we will be late for school.*
to put clothes on
2 *He was* **dressed** *in a black suit.*
to be attired in *He was* **attired in** *a black suit.*
to be wearing *He was* **wearing** *a black suit.*
to have on *He* **had** *a black suit on.*

drew verb past tense *see* draw

drink verb drinks, drinking, drank

1 *He picked up the glass of milk and* **drank** *it.*
Use **swallow** when someone drinks something quickly without tasting it: *She took a deep breath and* **swallowed** *the disgusting medicine.*

Use **sip** when someone drinks slowly: *She* **sipped** *the lovely cool apple juice.*

Use **gulp** or **swig** when someone drinks very quickly: *He* **gulped** *down a whole bottle of water.*

Use **guzzle** or **slurp** when someone drinks quickly and noisily: *She* **slurped** *the hot tea.*
2 *The dog* **drank** *its water.*
to lap up

drip verb

After the rain, water was **dripping** *from the trees above us.*
to drop
to splash
to trickle
to dribble

drive verb drives, driving, drove

1 *She got into her car and **drove** off.*

Use **speed** or **zoom** when someone drives quickly: *They **zoomed** along the road.*

Use **crawl** when someone drives slowly: *We **crawled** along behind the tractor.*

2 *She **drove** the car carefully into the parking space.*

to steer
to guide
to manoeuvre

drop noun

*I felt a few **drops** of rain on my face.*

a drip
a spot
a droplet

drop verb

*He accidentally **dropped** his glass.*

to let go of

drove verb past tense see drive

dry adjective

1 *The ground was very **dry**.*

hard
parched
arid
OPPOSITE **wet**

2 *They lived on **dry** bread and water.*

hard
stale

duck noun

a drake a male duck
a duckling a young duck

dug verb past tense see dig

dull adjective

1 *This television show is very **dull**.*

boring
tedious
uninteresting
OPPOSITE **interesting**

2 *She was wearing a **dull** green jumper.*

drab
dark
dreary
dowdy
OPPOSITE **bright**

3 *It was a rather **dull** day.*

grey
cloudy
overcast
dismal
miserable
OPPOSITE **bright**

dusty adjective

*The room was very **dusty**.*

dirty
mucky
filthy
OPPOSITE **clean**

duty noun

*It is your **duty** to look after the younger children.*

a responsibility
a job

a
b
c
d
e
f
g
h
i
j
k
l
m
n
o
p
q
r
s
t
u
v
w
x
y
z

Ee

eager adjective

*We were **eager** to go out and play.*

keen

impatient

anxious

OPPOSITE **reluctant**

earth noun

1 *This is the **earth** from space.*

the world

the globe

the planet

2 *Bulbs will start to grow when you plant them in the **earth**.*

the soil

the ground

easy adjective

*These sums were **easy** and we did them quickly.*

simple

straightforward

obvious

OPPOSITE **difficult**

eat verb eats, eating, ate

OVERUSED WORD

Here are some more interesting words for **eat**:

*Someone **ate** all the cake.*

Use **guzzle**, **polish off**, and **scoff** when someone eats something quickly: *We soon **polished off** the rest of the sandwiches.*

Use **wolf down**, **bolt**, **gobble**, and **devour** when someone eats something very quickly and greedily: *The hungry children **wolfed down** the pizza.*

Use **munch**, **crunch**, and **chomp** when someone eats noisily: *Alice **munched** noisily on an apple.*

Use **chew** and **suck** when someone eats something without biting it: *She was **sucking** a large ice lolly.*

Use **nibble** when someone eats something slowly, taking small bites: *She was **nibbling** on a slice of pizza.*

edge noun

1 *I bumped my leg on the **edge** of the table.*

the side

2 *There was a pattern around the **edge** of the plate.*

the outside

3 *The **edge** of the cup was cracked.*

the rim

4 *We walked right to the* **edge** *of the field.*
the boundary
5 *Keep close to the* **edge** *of the road when you are walking.*
the side
the verge
the kerb
6 *We live on the* **edge** *of the town.*
the outskirts
the suburbs

effect noun

What will be the **effect** *of the hot sun on these plants?*
the result
the impact
the consequence

effort noun

1 *You should put more* **effort** *into your spellings.*
work
2 *I made an* **effort** *to be cheerful.*
an attempt

elect verb

We **elect** *a new school captain each year.*
to choose
to pick
to vote for
to appoint

embarrassed adjective

I felt really **embarrassed** *about my mistake.*
uncomfortable
awkward
ashamed
shy
self-conscious

empty adjective

1 *There was an* **empty** *bottle on the table.*
unfilled
OPPOSITE **full**
2 *They've moved away, so their house is* **empty***.*
Use **unoccupied** or **vacant** if nobody is living in a house: *The house will be* **vacant** *next month, so we'll be able to move in.*
Use **bare** or **unfurnished** if there is nothing inside a room or house: *There was no furniture and the room was completely* **bare***.*
OPPOSITE **occupied**
3 *It was raining, so the town centre was* **empty***.*
deserted
OPPOSITE **crowded**

encourage verb

1 *My parents* **encouraged** *me to learn French.*
to persuade
to urge
2 *We all cheered to* **encourage** *our team.*
to support
to cheer on
to inspire
OPPOSITE **discourage**

end noun

1 *We walked right to the* **end** *of the lane.*
the limit
the boundary
2 *Please go to the* **end** *of the line.*
the back
the rear
3 *He tied a balloon to the* **end** *of the stick.*
the tip
the top
the bottom

4 *This book has a happy **end**.*
an ending
a finish
a conclusion

end verb
*When will the concert **end**?*
to stop
to finish
to conclude
Use **cease** when something finally ends, after a long time: *The rain finally **ceased**.*

enemy noun
*He fought bravely against his **enemy**.*
an opponent
a foe
a rival
OPPOSITE **friend**

energetic adjective
*I'm feeling quite **energetic** this morning and I'm going to go for a run.*
active
lively
full of beans

energy noun
*The children seem to have a lot of **energy** today.*
strength
stamina

enjoy verb
*I really **enjoyed** drinking my smoothie.*
to like
to love
to take pleasure from

enjoyable adjective
*It was a very **enjoyable** trip.*
pleasant
pleasurable
delightful
OPPOSITE **unpleasant**

enter verb
1 *She **entered** the house through the back door.*
to go into
to come into
to walk into
to run into
OPPOSITE **leave**
2 *Are you going to **enter** the competition?*
to go in for
to take part in
to join in

entertain verb
*The clown **entertained** the children.*
to amuse
to delight
to make someone laugh

enthusiastic adjective
*He is very **enthusiastic** about joining the basketball team.*
keen *He is **keen** to join the basketball team.*
eager *He is **eager** to join the basketball team.*

entrance noun
1 *We couldn't find the **entrance** to the building.*
the way in
the door
the gate
OPPOSITE **exit**

2 *They stood by the* **entrance** *to the cave.*
the mouth
the opening

equipment noun
We keep the games **equipment** *in the shed.*
things
gear *(informal)*
tackle
apparatus

escape verb
1 *The police arrived too late, and the robbers had* **escaped.**
to get away
to run away
to make your escape

To **break free** means to escape when you have been tied up or held: *Two policemen were holding him, but he managed to* **break free.**

To **give someone the slip** means to get away from someone who is following you: *I knew someone was following me, but I managed to* **give them the slip.**

2 *We went indoors to* **escape** *from the rain.*
to avoid

even adjective
1 *You need an* **even** *surface for road cycling.*
flat
smooth
level
OPPOSITE **uneven**
2 *Their scores were* **even** *at half time.*
equal
level
the same
OPPOSITE **different**

evening noun
We should be there by **evening.**
dusk
nightfall
sunset

event noun
1 *The party will be a big* **event.**
an occasion
2 *Some strange* **events** *have been happening lately.*
an incident

evil adjective
1 *I didn't think the witch in the story was* **evil.**
wicked
cruel
vile
2 *An* **evil** *king ruled over the land.*
wicked
bad
cruel
black-hearted
OPPOSITE **good**

exact adjective
Make sure you add the **exact** *amount of water.*
right
correct
precise

example noun
Can you show the other teachers an **example** *of your work?*
a sample
a specimen

A
B
C
D
E
F
G
H
I
J
K
L
M
N
O
P
Q
R
S
T
U
V
W
X
Y
Z

excellent adjective

*This is an **excellent** piece of work.*

very good
wonderful
brilliant *(informal)*
first-class
superb
outstanding
OPPOSITE **bad**

exchange verb

*I **exchanged** my old red bike for a new blue one.*

to change
to swap

excited adjective

*She was very **excited** because it was her birthday.*

happy
thrilled
enthusiastic
OPPOSITE **calm**

excitement noun

*I like films with a lot of **excitement**.*

action
activity
drama
suspense

exciting adjective

1 *We had a very **exciting** day at the zoo.*
thrilling
exhilarating
Use **action-packed** or **eventful** when a lot of different things happen: *We had an **action-packed** holiday.*

2 *I can't put this **exciting** book down.*
gripping
3 *It was a very **exciting** game to watch.*
fast-moving
tense
nail-biting
OPPOSITE **boring**

excuse verb

*Please **excuse** me for being late.*

to forgive
to pardon

exercise noun

*You should do more **exercise** to keep fit.*

sport
PE
games
running around

exhausted adjective

*I was **exhausted** after my long run.*

tired
worn out
shattered

expect verb

*I **expect** it will rain later as there are dark clouds in the sky.*

to think
to believe
to suppose

expensive adjective

*Those leggings are very **expensive** and I don't think I can afford them.*

dear
costly
OPPOSITE **cheap**

explain verb

*Alice **explained** how the machine worked.*

to describe

to show *She **showed** us how the machine worked.*

explode verb

1 *The fireworks **exploded** with a shower of stars.*

to go off

to burst

to go bang

2 *Don't put the tin in the microwave as it will **explode**.*

to blow up

explore verb

*Let's **explore** the cave.*

to look round

to search

to investigate

extra adjective

*I've brought some **extra** food in case we get hungry.*

more

additional

extraordinary adjective

*Standing before us was an **extraordinary** creature.*

strange

bizarre

incredible

remarkable

unusual

amazing

OPPOSITE **ordinary**

extreme adjective

*No plants can grow in the **extreme** heat of the desert.*

great

intense

severe

A
B
C
D
E
F
G
H
I
J
K
L
M
N
O
P
Q
R
S
T
U
V
W
X
Y
Z

Ff

face noun
The little boy had a sad face.
an expression

fact noun
We found out some interesting facts about the ancient Romans.
information
data

fade verb
1 *The colour in my dress has faded from a dark to a light blue.*
to become lighter
2 *It was evening, and the light was beginning to fade.*
to go
to dwindle
to grow dim
3 *The sound of the engine gradually faded as the car moved further away.*
to become faint
to disappear
to die away

fail verb
Our attempt to launch the boat failed.
to be unsuccessful
to meet with disaster

failure noun
The magician's trick was a complete failure!
a disaster
a flop
OPPOSITE **success**

faint adjective
1 *Alice heard the faint noise of music coming from the house next door.*
quiet
weak
muffled
dim
OPPOSITE **loud**
2 *The writing was quite faint and difficult to read.*
unclear
indistinct
faded
OPPOSITE **clear**

faint verb
I fainted because it was so hot.
to pass out
to lose consciousness

fair adjective
1 *Ben has fair hair.*
light
golden
blond for a boy
blonde for a girl
OPPOSITE **dark**
2 *It's not fair if she gets more sweets than me.*
right
reasonable
OPPOSITE **unfair**
3 *I don't think the referee was very fair.*
impartial
unbiased
honest
OPPOSITE **biased**
4 *We've got a fair chance of winning.*
reasonable
good
moderate

fall verb falls, falling, fell

1 *Watch you don't **fall** over the step.*

Use **trip** or **stumble** when someone falls because their foot catches on something: *I **tripped** over one of the wires.*

Use **slip** when someone falls on a slippery surface: *I **slipped** on the ice.*

Use **tumble** when someone falls from a height: *He **tumbled** off the wall.*

Use **plunge** when someone falls into water: *She couldn't stop running and plunged head first into the pond.*

Use **lose your balance** when someone falls after they have been balancing on something: *I **lost my balance** halfway across the tightrope.*

2 *The book fell off the table.*

to drop

to tumble

Use **crash** when something makes a loud noise as it falls: *The pile of plates **crashed** to the floor.*

3 *Snow began to fall.*

to come down

false adjective

1 *He was wearing a **false** beard as a disguise.*

fake

artificial

pretend

OPPOSITE **real**

2 *I was given **false** information about the school trip.*

incorrect

misleading

OPPOSITE **correct**

famous adjective

*One day Ben might be a **famous** pop star.*

well-known

world-famous

celebrated

OPPOSITE **unknown**

fan noun

*Are you a hockey **fan**?*

a supporter

a follower

an admirer

fantastic adjective

*We had a **fantastic** time at the concert.*

wonderful

brilliant (informal)

great

fabulous

marvellous

sensational

OPPOSITE **terrible**

farm noun

WORD WEB

*Some types of **farm**:*

an arable farm one that grows crops

a dairy farm one that keeps cows

a fruit farm

a poultry farm one with chickens, ducks, or turkeys

a ranch a cattle farm in North America

a smallholding a small farm

fashion noun

*These blue shoes are the latest **fashion**.*

a style

a trend

a craze

a look

a
b
c
d
e
f
g
h
i
j
k
l
m
n
o
p
q
r
s
t
u
v
w
x
y
z

A B C D E **F** G H I J K L M N O P Q R S T U V W X Y Z

fashionable adjective

1 *He wears very* **fashionable** *clothes.*

trendy

stylish

2 *These coats are* **fashionable** *at the moment.*

popular

in fashion

all the rage *(informal)*

OPPOSITE **unfashionable**

fast adjective

1 *He's a very* **fast** *runner.*

quick

speedy

swift

2 *He loves driving* **fast** *cars.*

powerful

3 *We'll go on the* **fast** *train.*

high-speed

express

4 *Scientists are working on a new* **fast** *aeroplane.*

supersonic faster than the speed of sound

5 *We were walking at quite a* **fast** *pace.*

brisk

quick

swift

OPPOSITE **slow**

fast adverb

She was walking quite **fast**.

quickly

rapidly

swiftly

fasten verb

1 *Please remember to* **fasten** *your seat belt.*

to do up

to buckle

2 *Ben stopped to* **fasten** *his shoelaces.*

to tie up

to do up

3 **Fasten** *the two bits of string together.*

to tie

to fix

to join

to secure

fat adjective

The ticket collector was a little **fat** *man.*

Use **plump**, **tubby**, **chubby**, or **podgy** for someone who is slightly fat in a nice way: *In the pushchair was a* **chubby**, *smiling baby.*

Use **stout** or **portly** for an older person who is quite fat: *My uncle Bill likes his food, and as a result he's rather* **stout**.

Use **overweight** or **obese** for someone who is so fat that they are unhealthy: *If you don't do enough exercise, you can become* **obese**.

OPPOSITE **thin**

favourite adjective

What is your **favourite** *book?*

best-loved

number-one

fear noun

He didn't want to sing in the concert and I could see **fear** *in his eyes.*

Use **terror** for a very strong feeling of fear: *Emily screamed in* **terror** *as the ogre came towards her.*

Use **panic** for a sudden feeling of fear when you are so frightened that you don't know what to do: *A feeling of* **panic** *came over me as our little boat began to sink.*

Use **dread** or **horror** for a feeling of fear and disgust: *He watched in* **horror** *as the huge snake slid towards him.*

feel verb feels, feeling, felt

1 *She put out her hand and* **felt** *the puppy's fur.*

to touch
to stroke

2 *I* **felt** *that I was in the right.*

to believe
to think

feeling noun

1 *Try to think about other people's* **feelings.**

an emotion

2 *I had a* **feeling** *that somebody was following me*

a sensation

fell verb past tense *see* **fall**

felt verb past tense *see* **feel**

festival noun

Diwali is a Hindu religious **festival.**

a celebration

fetch verb

1 **Fetch** *your bag from the cloakroom.*

to get
to bring

2 *I'll come and* **fetch** *you at five o'clock.*

to collect
to pick up

fiction noun

I like to read **fiction.**

stories
tales
myths
legends
fantasies

field noun

The ponies have their own **field** *behind the house.*

a paddock
an enclosure
a meadow

fierce adjective

Tigers are very **fierce** *animals.*

ferocious
savage
aggressive
dangerous

fight verb fight, fighting, fought

1 *The tigers began to* **fight.**

to brawl
to wrestle
to grapple

2 *Why are you two children always* **fighting?**

to argue
to quarrel
to bicker

fight noun

The two boys had a **fight** *after school.*

Use **brawl** or **punch-up** for a small fight: *The argument between the two boys ended up as a* **punch-up**.

Use **battle** or **clash** for a big fight between a lot of people: *Many* **battles** *were fought during the war.*

fill verb

1 *We* **filled** *the boxes with toys.*

to pack
to load
to stuff
to cram

a b c d e **f** g h i j k l m n o p q r s t u v w x y z

A
B
C
D
E
F
G
H
I
J
K
L
M
N
O
P
Q
R
S
T
U
V
W
X
Y
Z

2 *They* **filled** *the huge balloon with air.*
to inflate
OPPOSITE **empty**

film noun
We watched a **film** *on TV last night.*
a movie

> **WORD WEB**
>
> *Some types of* **film**:
> **an action film**
> **an adventure film**
> **a cartoon**
> **a comedy**
> **a documentary** a film that gives you information about something
> **a horror film**
> **an thriller**
> **a western** a film about cowboys

filthy adjective
1 *The footballers were* **filthy** *by the end of the game.*
dirty
muddy
mucky
grubby
grimy
2 *The room was* **filthy** *and hadn't been cleaned for months.*
dirty
dusty
messy
3 *The water in this river is* **filthy** *and brown.*
polluted
OPPOSITE **clean**

finally adverb
We **finally** *arrived home at seven o'clock.*
eventually
at last

find verb finds, finding, found
1 *I can't* **find** *my homework in my bedroom although I'm sure I put it there.*
to locate
OPPOSITE **lose**
2 *The children* **found** *an old map in the attic.*
to discover
to come across
to stumble upon
to notice
to spot
3 *I lost my cat but* **found** *her in the neighbour's garden.*
to trace
to track down
4 *When the archaeologists started digging, they* **found** *some very interesting things.*
to dig up
to uncover
to unearth

fine adjective
1 *You will need to use a very* **fine** *thread.*
thin
delicate
light
OPPOSITE **thick**
2 *I hope the weather is* **fine** *for sports day.*
sunny
dry
bright
clear
cloudless
OPPOSITE **dull**

3 *I felt ill yesterday, but today I feel* **fine.**

okay

all right

OPPOSITE **ill**

4 *The town hall is a very* **fine** *building.*

beautiful

magnificent

splendid

finish verb

1 *What time will the party* **finish***?*

to end

to stop

2 *Have you* **finished** *your homework?*

to complete

to do

3 *Hurry up and* **finish** *your meal.*

to eat

to eat up

4 *I haven't* **finished** *my drink.*

to drink

to drink up

OPPOSITE **start**

fire noun

1 *We lit a match to start the* **fire.**

a bonfire *a fire outside*

2 *The explosion caused a huge* **fire.**

a blaze

an inferno

fire verb

They were **firing** *at a row of bottles on the wall.*

to shoot

firm adjective

1 *The ladder didn't feel very* **firm.**

stable

secure

steady

solid

OPPOSITE **unsteady**

2 *We patted the sand down until it was* **firm.**

hard

rigid

OPPOSITE **soft**

first adjective

1 *We were the* **first** *to arrive at the party.*

earliest

soonest

2 *Who designed the* **first** *aeroplane?*

earliest

original

fit adjective

1 *You have to be* **fit** *to run a marathon.*

strong

healthy

well

OPPOSITE **unfit**

2 *I don't think this food is* **fit** *to eat.*

suitable

good enough

OPPOSITE **unsuitable**

fit verb

1 *These shoes* **fit** *me very well.*

to be the right size *These shoes are the right size for me.*

2 *This huge box won't* **fit** *in the back of the car.*

to go

A B C D E F G H I J K L M N O P Q R S T U V W X Y Z

fix verb

1 *Mum **fixed** the shelves onto the wall so I had somewhere to put my books.*

to attach
to tie
to stick
to nail
to fasten

2 *Our TV is broken and we can't **fix** it.*

to mend
to repair

flat adjective

*You need a nice **flat** surface to work on.*

level
even
smooth
horizontal
OPPOSITE **uneven**

flew verb past tense see **fly**

flow verb

*Water was **flowing** quickly along the pipe.*

Use **pour**, **stream**, **gush**, and **spurt** when water flows very quickly: *The side of the pool split and water came **gushing** out.*

Use **drip** and **trickle** when water flows very slowly: *Water was **dripping** from the tap and keeping us awake at night.*

Use **leak** when water flows through a small hole in something: *Water was **leaking** into the house through a hole in the roof.*

Use **gurgle**, **burble**, and **babble** when water flows noisily over stones: *A little stream **babbled** under the bridge.*

flower noun

*We admired the **flowers** on the rose bush.*

a bloom
blossom

sunflowers

WORD WEB

Some garden flowers:
anemones
bougainvillea
carnations
crocuses
daffodils
geraniums
hibiscus
jasmine
lavender
lilac
lilies
marigolds
pansies
petunia

roses
snowdrops
sunflowers
sweet peas
tulips
wallflowers

Some wild flowers:
bluebells
buttercups
daisies
dandelions
foxgloves
poppies
primroses

fluffy adjective

*She picked up the small, **fluffy** kitten.*

furry
soft
woolly

fly verb flies, flying, flew

*We watched the birds **flying** high above our heads.*

Use **glide** when something moves quietly through the sky: *A hot-air balloon **glided** silently past us.*

Use **soar** when a bird or plane flies high in the sky: *The eagle **soared** high above us.*

Use **hover** when something stays in the same place in the air: *A helicopter **hovered** over the field.*

Use **flutter**, **flit**, and **dart** when something flies about quickly: *Bats were **flitting** about in the barn.*

Use **swoop** or **dive** when something flies down towards the ground: *The owl **swooped** down onto its prey.*

fold verb
Fold the paper along the dotted line.
to bend
to crease

follow verb
1 *Our friends **followed** us to the campsite.*
Use **chase**, **run after**, and **pursue** when someone is trying to catch a person: *The police **pursued** the two robbers.*

Use **shadow** and **tail** when someone follows a person secretly: *We **tailed** the teacher as far as the library.*

Use **track** when someone follows the tracks that a person has left: *They brought in dogs to **track** the criminals.*

2 Follow *this road until you come to a crossroads.*
to take
to go along
to continue along

3 Follow *my instructions carefully.*
to pay attention to
to obey

food noun
1 *We were all tired, thirsty, and in need of **food**.*
something to eat
refreshments

nourishment
grub (informal)
a meal

2 *We've got plenty of **food** for the animals.*
feed
fodder

fool noun
*Don't be such a **fool** and put your jacket on when you go out!*
an idiot
a twit
an imbecile
a clown

fool verb
*You can't **fool** me.*
to trick
to deceive

foolish adjective
*I was **foolish** to forget to my homework.*
silly
stupid
daft
mad (informal)
idiotic
unwise
OPPOSITE **sensible**

foot noun
a paw a dog's or cat's foot
a hoof a horse's foot
a trotter a pig's foot

force noun
*We had to use **force** to open the door.*
strength
might
power

A B C D E **F** G H I J K L M N O P Q R S T U V W X Y Z

force verb

1 *He forced me to give him money.*

to make *He made me give him the money.*

to order *He ordered me to give him the money.*

2 *They forced the door open.*

to push

to break

to smash

forest noun

There are lots of large trees in the forest.

a wood

a jungle *a tropical forest*

forget verb forgets, forgetting, forgot

I forgot my PE kit.

to leave behind *I've left my PE kit behind.*

to not bring *I haven't brought my PE kit.*

OPPOSITE remember

forgot verb past tense *see* forget

form noun

1 *The bicycle is a form of transport.*

a type

a sort

a kind

2 *He is a magician who can change himself into any form he chooses.*

a shape

form verb

These rocks formed millions of years ago.

to develop

to be made *These rocks were made millions of years ago.*

fought verb past tense *see* fight

foul adjective

There was a foul, rotten smell in the kitchen.

horrible

disgusting

nasty

revolting

repulsive

found verb past tense *see* find

fragile adjective

Be careful, these glasses are fragile.

delicate

flimsy

breakable

brittle

OPPOSITE strong

free adjective

1 *At last he was free!*

at liberty

out of prison

2 *If you buy a book, you get a free pencil.*

for nothing

complimentary

free verb

Ben was freed from detention at four o'clock.

to release

to liberate

to set free

fresh adjective

1 *Start each answer on a fresh page.*

clean

new

different

2 *I love the taste of fresh strawberries.*

freshly picked

3 *We had* **fresh** *bread for tea.*

warm

freshly baked

4 *The* **fresh** *air will do you good.*

clean

clear

pure

bracing

5 *I felt lovely and* **fresh** *after my swim.*

lively

energetic

refreshed

invigorated

friend noun

A **mate** or **pal** is quite an informal way of saying a friend: *Who's your best* **mate**?

A **companion** is someone you travel with or do things with: *I took my dog with me as a travelling* **companion**.

A **partner** or **colleague** is someone you work with: *I always choose Samir as my* **partner** *in class.*

An **ally** is someone who helps you in a fight: *I needed an* **ally** *in my fight with the Jones boys.*

friendly adjective

1 *Alice is a very* **friendly** *person and is nice to everyone.*

kind

nice

pleasant

amiable

affectionate

2 *Don't worry, our dog is very* **friendly** *and really likes people.*

good-natured

gentle

3 *Tina and I are quite* **friendly** *now.*

pally *(informal)*

matey *(informal)*

close

OPPOSITE **unfriendly**

frighten verb

The noise downstairs **frightened** *us.*

to scare

Use **startle**, **shock**, or **make someone jump** if something frightens you suddenly: *Sam* **startled** *me when he jumped out from behind a bush.*

Use **terrify** if something frightens you a lot: *That story* **terrified** *me when I was young.*

frightened adjective

Are you **frightened** *of spiders?*

afraid

scared

Use **startled** if you are frightened by something sudden: *I was* **startled** *when the door suddenly opened.*

Use **terrified** or **petrified** if you are very frightened: *James was* **petrified** *when he saw the lion.*

frightening adjective

The movie was quite **frightening** *and I was too scared to sleep after watching it.*

scary

Use **terrifying** for something that is very frightening: *It was* **terrifying** *going on such a big roller coaster.*

front noun

At last we got to the **front** *of the queue.*

the beginning

the head

OPPOSITE **back**

a
b
c
d
e
f
g
h
i
j
k
l
m
n
o
p
q
r
s
t
u
v
w
x
y
z

A B C D E F G H I J K L M N O P Q R S T U V W X Y Z

fruit noun

WORD WEB

Some **fruits:**

gooseberries

raisins

a peach

a tangerine

grapes

a passion fruit

a banana

a tomato

an orange

a raspberry

a plum

an apple

a lemon

dates

a star fruit

a pear

a blackberry

cherries

a kiwi fruit

a nectarine

a strawberry

an apricot

a nut

a mango

a pineapple

rhubarb

a grapefruit

a melon

full adjective

1 *We poured water into the bucket until it was **full**.*

full to the brim
overflowing

2 *The school hall was **full**.*

packed
full to capacity

3 *The room was **full** of people.*

crowded
packed

4 *The basket was **full** of good things to eat.*

packed with
crammed with
bursting with
bulging with
OPPOSITE **empty**

fun noun

*We had lots of **fun** on the beach.*

enjoyment
pleasure

funny adjective

1 *He told us a very **funny** joke and we laughed for ages.*

amusing

Use **hilarious** for something that is very funny: *The comedian was absolutely **hilarious**.*

Use **witty** for something that is funny and clever: *Joe's very good at making **witty** jokes.*
OPPOSITE **serious**

2 *We had to write a **funny** poem.*

humorous

3 *You look really **funny** in that hat.*

comical
ridiculous

4 *This sauce tastes very **funny**.*

strange
peculiar
odd
curious

furious adjective

*My dad was **furious** when he saw the mess.*

livid
fuming

furry adjective

*The bear's **furry** coat looked soft and warm.*

fluffy
woolly
soft

fussy adjective

1 *Some children are quite **fussy** about their food.*

choosy
picky
hard to please

2 *My sister is very **fussy** about keeping her room neat and tidy.*

particular
fastidious

a
b
c
d
e
f
g
h
i
j
k
l
m
n
o
p
q
r
s
t
u
v
w
x
y
z

77

ABCDEFGHIJKLMNOPQRSTUVWXYZ

Gg

game noun
Alice played a game of hopscotch.
a match
a tournament
a competition
a contest

gang noun
Do you want to join our gang?
a group
a crowd
a band

gather verb
1 *People gathered round to watch the jugglers.*
to crowd round
to come together
to assemble

2 *We gathered blackberries from the fields.*
to pick
to collect
3 *I need to gather some information for my project.*
to collect
to find

gave verb past tense *see* **give**

general adjective
The general opinion in our class is that school is fun.
common
popular
widespread

generous adjective
My grandma is a very generous person, and she always gives us presents.
kind
unselfish
big-hearted
OPPOSITE selfish

gentle adjective
1 *Anna is very gentle with the baby animals at the farm.*
kind
quiet
good-tempered
sweet-tempered
loving
tender
2 *I gave her a gentle tap on the shoulder.*
light
soft
OPPOSITE rough

get verb gets, getting, got

OVERUSED WORD

Here are some more interesting words for **get**:

1 *I got a new bike for my birthday.*
to receive
to be given
2 *Where can I get some paper?*
to find
to obtain
3 *We're going to the shop to get some food.*
to buy
to purchase
4 *How much money do you get for doing the paper round?*
to earn
to receive
5 *I wonder who will get the first prize.*
to win

6 *Our team got 15 points.*
to score
7 *I'll go and get the drinks.*
to fetch
to bring
8 *I got chickenpox last winter.*
to catch
9 *What time will we get home?*
to arrive
to reach
to come
10 *It's getting colder.*
to become
to grow
to turn

ghost noun

Have you ever seen a ghost?

a phantom
an apparition
a spirit
a spook

giggle verb

The girls were all giggling.

to snigger
to chuckle

girl noun

a lass
a kid
a child
a youngster
a teenager

give verb gives, giving, gave

OVERUSED WORD

Here are some more interesting words for **give**:

1 *Mia gave me a book.*
to hand
to pass
2 *I gave Rebecca a CD for her birthday.*
to buy
3 *The school gives us pens and paper.*
to provide
to supply
4 *The judges gave first prize to Samir.*
to award
to present
5 *We gave our old toys to the charity.*
to donate

a b c d e f **g** h i j k l m n o p q r s t u v w x y z

A
B
C
D
E
F
G
H
I
J
K
L
M
N
O
P
Q
R
S
T
U
V
W
X
Y
Z

glad adjective

I'm glad you got here safely.

pleased

relieved

happy

Use **delighted** if you are very glad about something: *We were delighted when we won the competition.*

go verb goes, going, went

OVERUSED WORD

Here are some more interesting words for **go**:

1 *Let's go along this path.*

to walk

Use **run**, **rush**, **hurry**, or **race** when you go somewhere very quickly: *I rushed home as fast as I could.*

Use **march** or **stride** when you go along taking big steps: *Mr Hoggett strode angrily towards the house.*

Use **saunter** or **stroll** when you go along slowly, in a relaxed way: *In the afternoon, we strolled through the park.*

Use **creep**, **sneak**, or **tiptoe** when you go somewhere quietly or secretly: *I sneaked out of the class when no one was looking.*

2 *We went along the road for a few miles.*

to drive

to travel

to speed

3 *We're going at six o'clock.*

to leave

to set out

4 *This road goes to London.*

to lead

5 *When we got back, our suitcases had gone.*

to disappear

to vanish

6 *My watch doesn't go.*

to work

7 *When the teacher talks, all of the children go quiet.*

to become

to grow

go down

Go down the stairs.

to descend

go into

Go into the kitchen.

to enter

go out of

Go out of the house.

to leave

to exit

go up

Go up the stairs.

to climb

to ascend

good adjective

OVERUSED WORD

Here are some more interesting words for **good**:

1 *This is a really **good** book.*

Use **wonderful**, **brilliant** (*informal*), **excellent**, **fantastic**, or **great** if something is very good: *He told us some **wonderful** stories about his travels.*

Use **enjoyable**, **exciting**, or **interesting** for something you enjoy a lot: *We had a very **enjoyable** time at the seaside.*

Use **amusing** or **entertaining** for something that makes you laugh: *It was a very **entertaining** story.*

2 *William is a very good footballer.*
- skilful
- talented
- competent

3 *I hope the weather is **good** for our school sports day.*
- fine
- nice
- dry
- sunny
- warm

4 *Jessica has got a very **good** imagination.*
- lively
- vivid

5 *He gave the police a **good** description of the thief.*
- clear
- vivid
- precise

6 *You have been a very **good** friend to me.*
- kind
- caring
- loving
- loyal

7 *The children have been very **good** all day.*
- well-behaved
- polite

OPPOSITE **bad**

got verb past tense *see* get

grab verb

1 *I **grabbed** my coat and ran out as I was late for the party.*
- to seize
- to snatch
- to pick up

2 *Tom **grabbed** my arm forcefully.*
- to take hold of
- to grasp
- to clutch
- to grip

graceful adjective

*She is a very **graceful** dancer.*
- elegant
- beautiful
- smooth

OPPOSITE **clumsy**

grateful adjective

*We are very **grateful** for all your help.*
- thankful
- appreciative *We are very **appreciative** of all your help.*

OPPOSITE **ungrateful**

a b c d e f **g** h i j k l m n o p q r s t u v w x y z

A
B
C
D
E
F
G
H
I
J
K
L
M
N
O
P
Q
R
S
T
U
V
W
X
Y
Z

great adjective

1 *The **great** hall was used for a banquet scene in a movie.*

big
large
enormous
huge
vast
OPPOSITE **small**

2 *The royal wedding was a **great** occasion.*

grand
magnificent
splendid
OPPOSITE **unimportant**

3 *He was a **great** musician.*

famous
well-known
celebrated
OPPOSITE **terrible**

4 *It's a **great** book!*

wonderful
brilliant (informal)
excellent
fantastic
OPPOSITE **terrible**

green adjective

*She was wearing a **green** dress.*

emerald
lime green bright green
bottle green dark green

grew verb past tense see grow

grey adjective

1 *The sky was **grey** and it looked like it was about to rain.*

cloudy
dull
overcast
grim
forbidding

2 *They met an old man with **grey** hair.*

white
silver

grin verb

*Samir **grinned** when Ben asked if he'd like to read his comic.*

to smile
to beam

grip verb

*The old lady **gripped** my arm tightly.*

to hold on to
to grasp
to clutch

groan verb

*We all **groaned** when the teacher told us we had to stay inside.*

to moan
to sigh
to protest

ground noun

1 *Don't leave your bags on the wet* **ground.**

soil

earth

2 *Who owns the piece of* **ground** *next to the church?*

land

territory

group noun

1 *There was a large* **group** *of people waiting outside the arena.*

a crowd

a throng

Use **mob** for a large, noisy group: *There was an angry* **mob** *outside the school.*

2 *He was showing a* **group** *of tourists round the museum.*

a party

3 *We met up with a* **group** *of our friends.*

a bunch

a crowd

a gang

4 *What's your favourite pop* **group**?

a band

group verb

We had to **group** *the poems together according to their author.*

to arrange

to classify

to sort

to order

grow verb grows, growing, grew

1 *The sunflowers* **grew** *very tall this year.*

to get bigger

to get taller

to shoot up

2 *The seeds are starting to* **grow.**

Use **germinate** or **sprout** when seeds first start to grow: *After three or four days the seeds will start to* **germinate.**

Use **shoot up** or **spring up** when the plant starts to grow taller: *Weeds were* **springing up** *all over the garden.*

3 *The number of children in our school is* **growing.**

to increase

4 *We* **grow** *vegetables in our garden.*

to plant

to produce

grown-up noun

Ask a **grown-up** *if you need help.*

an adult

grown-up adjective

You need to behave in a **grown-up** *manner.*

mature

responsible

sensible

grumble verb

Stop **grumbling** *about how much homework you have to do!*

to complain

to moan

to whinge

to whine

grumpy adjective

Why are you so **grumpy** *today?*

cross

bad-tempered

sulky

moody

OPPOSITE good-tempered

A B C D E F **G** H I J K L M N O P Q R S T U V W X Y Z

guard verb

1 *Soldiers* **guard** *the castle against attack.*
to protect
to defend
to watch
2 *A mother elephant will* **guard** *her young.*
to look after
to watch over
to protect

guard noun

There was a **guard** *by the door.*
a sentry
a lookout
a security officer in a bank, office, or shop

guess verb

1 *Can you* **guess** *how many sweets are in the jar?*
to estimate
2 *Because they were late, I* **guessed** *that their car must have broken down.*
to think
to suppose
to predict
to infer

guide verb

He **guided** *us through the wood to the main road.*
to lead
to steer
to escort
to accompany

guilty adjective

I felt **guilty** *because I had been horrible to my sister.*
bad
ashamed
sorry
remorseful
sheepish
OPPOSITE **innocent**

Hh

had verb past tense *see* **have**

hair noun

*She had blonde **hair**.*

Use **locks** for long hair and **curls** for curly hair: *She looked in the mirror and admired her golden **locks**.*

🕷 WORD WEB

Some words you might use to describe someone's **hair**:	Some words you might use to describe the colour of someone's **hair**:
beautiful	auburn
bobbed	black
curly	blond(e)
dishevelled	brown
fine	chestnut
frizzy	dark
glossy	ebony
long	fair
matted	ginger
scruffy	golden
shiny	grey
short	jet black
sleek	mousy
straight	red
thick	sandy
tousled	strawberry blond(e)
untidy	white
wavy	
wispy	
windswept	

---

hairy adjective

*They were greeted by a large, **hairy** dog.*

furry
shaggy
woolly

handsome adjective

*He is a very **handsome** man.*

good-looking
attractive

Use **gorgeous** for a man who is very handsome: *He's my favourite actor—he's absolutely **gorgeous**!*

OPPOSITE ugly

hang verb hangs, hanging, hung

1 *A bunch of keys **hung** from the keyring.*

to dangle
to swing

2 *We **hung** the picture on the wall.*

to attach
to fasten
to fix

3 *He was **hanging** on to the rope.*

to hold on to
to cling on to

happen verb

*At what time of day did the power cut **happen**?*

to take place
to occur

A B C D E F G **H** I J K L M N O P Q R S T U V W X Y Z

happy adjective

OVERUSED WORD

Here are some more interesting words for **happy**:

*I'm feeling very **happy** today.*

Use **cheerful**, **contented**, or **good-humoured** if you are in a good mood and not grumpy or upset about anything: *Sarah is a very **cheerful** person who's always smiling.*

Use **pleased** or **glad** if you are happy about something that has happened: *I'll be very **glad** when this adventure is over!*

Use **delighted**, **thrilled**, or **overjoyed** if you are very happy: *Everyone was **overjoyed** when the children were found safe and well.*

OPPOSITE **unhappy**

hard adjective

OVERUSED WORD

Here are some more interesting words for **hard**:

1 *The ground was **hard** and frozen.*

firm

solid

rigid

OPPOSITE **soft**

2 *The teacher gave us some very **hard** sums to do.*

difficult

complicated

tricky

challenging

OPPOSITE **easy**

3 *Carrying the bricks was very **hard** work.*

tiring

exhausting

strenuous

back-breaking

OPPOSITE **easy**

hardly adverb

*I was so tired I could **hardly** walk.*

scarcely

barely

only just

harm verb

1 *I didn't mean to **harm** you.*

to hurt

to injure

to wound

2 *Smoking can **harm** your health.*

to damage

to ruin

harsh adjective

1 *The machine made a **harsh** sound.*

Use **rough** or **grating** for a low sound: *The wheel made a loud **grating** sound as it turned.*

Use **shrill** or **piercing** for a high sound: *They heard a **piercing** scream.*

OPPOSITE **gentle**

2 *That punishment seemed a bit **harsh**.*

hard

severe
strict
unkind
OPPOSITE **lenient**

has verb past tense see **have**

hat noun

hate verb
*I **hate** cold weather!*
to dislike
to detest
to loathe
to not be able to stand *I can't stand
cold weather!*
OPPOSITE **love**

a b c d e f g **h** i j k l m n o p q r s t u v w x y z

WORD WEB

*Some **hats**:*
a baseball cap
a beanie
a beret
a boater
a bonnet
a cap
a fedora
a helmet
a panama
a riding hat
a straw hat
a sun hat
a turban
a woolly hat
a witch's hat

a pirate hat

a clown hat

a helmet

a bowler hat

a cap

a top hat

a cone hat

a sombrero

have verb has, having, had

1 *Our school* **has** *a smartboard in every classroom.*

to own

to possess

2 *I don't need this book now. You can* **have** *it.*

to keep

3 *I* **had** *some lovely presents for my birthday.*

to get

to receive

4 *My brother* **has** *chickenpox.*

to be suffering from

to be infected with *He* **is infected with** *chickenpox.*

healthy adjective

1 *Most of the children here are very* **healthy** *and well.*

strong

well

fit

2 *This food is very* **healthy** *and delicious.*

nutritious

nourishing

good for you

OPPOSITE **unhealthy**

heap noun

There was a **heap** *of dirty clothes on the floor.*

a pile

a mound

a mass

a stack

hear verb hears, hearing, heard

1 *I couldn't* **hear** *my music as people were talking very loudly.*

to make out

to catch

2 *Have you* **heard** *the band's new single?*

to listen to

heard verb past tense *see* **hear**

heat noun

I could feel the **heat** *from the fire.*

warmth

heat verb

We can **heat** *up a pizza for lunch.*

to warm up

heavy adjective

This bag is very **heavy** *and I can't lift it.*

weighty

OPPOSITE **light**

held verb past tense *see* **hold**

help verb

1 *Shall I* **help** *you with your bags?*

to assist

to lend a hand

to give someone a hand

2 *The team must all* **help** *one another.*

to support

to cooperate with

help noun

Do you need some **help***?*

assistance

advice

support

helpful adjective

She is always very **helpful** *in class.*

kind

considerate

willing

OPPOSITE **unhelpful**

helping noun

*He gave me a huge **helping** of chips.*

a portion
a serving

hid verb past tense *see* hide

hide verb hides, hiding, hid

1 *We **hid** in the garden shed.*

to keep out of sight

Use **go into hiding** when someone hides for a long time: *The robbers **went into hiding** for several weeks after the theft.*

Use **lie low** when someone tries to avoid certain people: *I knew Mrs Flint would be furious with me, so I decided to **lie low** for a week or two.*

2 *They **hid** the old coins in a hollow tree.*

to conceal
to stash

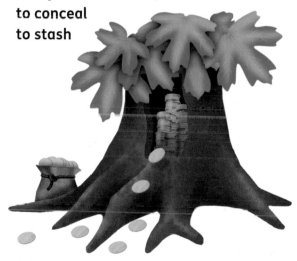

high adjective

1 *There are a lot of **high** buildings in the city.*

tall
big
towering

2 *Some shops charge very **high** prices.*

inflated
exorbitant

3 *She spoke in a **high** voice.*

high-pitched
squeaky
piercing

Use **piercing** or **shrill** for a loud, unpleasant high voice: *'Get out!' she cried in a **shrill** voice.*

OPPOSITE **low**

hill noun

*We walked up the **hill**.*

a mountain
a slope

hit verb hits, hitting, hit

1 *You mustn't **hit** people as you might hurt them.*

to strike

To **punch** or **thump** someone means to hit them with your fist: *'Get out of my way, or I'll **thump** you!' he shouted.*

To **slap** someone means to hit them with your open hand: *She **slapped** the other girl.*

To **smack** someone means to hit them as a punishment: *Some parents **smack** their children.*

To **beat** or **thrash** someone means to hit them many times with a stick: *The cruel master used to **beat** the horses.*

2 *I fell and **hit** my elbow on the pavement.*

to knock
to bang
to bash
to bump

3 *The car went out of control and **hit** a wall.*

to bump into
to crash into
to smash into
to collide with

a b c d e f g **h** i j k l m n o p q r s t u v w x y z

4 *He* **hit** *the ball as hard as he could.*
to strike
to whack

hobby noun

Skateboarding is my favourite **hobby.**
a pastime
an interest
an activity
a leisure activity

hold verb holds, holding, held

1 *Can I* **hold** *the baby?*
to carry
to cuddle
to hug
to cradle
2 *She* **held** *the handrail tightly.*
to grip
to grasp
to clutch
3 *One of the boys was* **holding** *a stick.*
to brandish
to wield
4 *This box* **holds** *20 pencils.*
to take
to contain
to have space for *This box* **has space for** *20 pencils.*

hole noun

1 *We climbed through a* **hole** *in the hedge.*
an opening
a gap
a space
2 *There was a big* **hole** *in the ground.*
a pit
a crater
a chasm

3 *I could see them through a* **hole** *in the wall.*
a crack
a slit
a chink
4 *There's a* **hole** *in my shirt.*
a split
a rip
a tear
5 *There was a* **hole** *in one of the water pipes.*
a crack
a leak
6 *One of my bicycle tyres has a* **hole** *in it.*
a puncture
7 *The tiny animal escaped back into its* **hole.**
a burrow
a den
a nest

home noun

This is the **home** *that I have lived in for years.*
a residence
a house
a flat
an apartment

honest adjective

1 *I'm sure he is an* **honest** *boy who never lies.*
good
trustworthy
OPPOSITE **dishonest**
2 *Did you enjoy the film? Be* **honest.**
truthful
sincere
frank

hopeless adjective

I'm **hopeless** *at swimming.*
bad
no good

terrible
useless
incompetent
OPPOSITE **good**

horrible adjective

1 *Don't be* **horrible**! *It isn't nice.*
nasty
unpleasant
mean
unkind
obnoxious
horrid

2 *I can't eat this food. It's* **horrible**.
revolting
disgusting
tasteless
inedible

3 *I don't like that* **horrible** *jumper!*
vile
hideous
repulsive

4 *The weather was* **horrible** *and we stayed in.*
awful
dreadful
terrible
appalling

5 *I had a dream about a* **horrible** *monster.*
terrible
frightening
terrifying
OPPOSITE **pleasant**

horror noun

The sight of the huge beast filled me with horror.
fear
terror
dread

horse noun

a pony
a nag an old horse
a mare a female horse
a stallion a male horse
a foal a baby horse
a colt a young horse

WORD WEB

Some types of **horse**:

a carthorse	**a Shetland pony**
a racehorse	**a Shire horse**

Some words you might use to describe the colour of a **horse**:

black
bay reddish brown
chestnut
dapple grey
roan brown or black, with some white hairs
palomino gold coat with white mane
piebald with patches of different colours
skewbald with patches of white and another colour
white

WRITING TIPS

Here are some useful words for writing about **horses**:

- *The little pony* **trotted** *down the lane.*
- *The stallion* **cantered** *across the field.*
- *The racehorse* **galloped** *towards the finishing line.*
- *The foal* **neighed** *excitely.*

They urged their horses into a canter over the bridge. — Martin Conway, *Olaf the Viking Pig who would be King*

a
b
c
d
e
f
g
h
i
j
k
l
m
n
o
p
q
r
s
t
u
v
w
x
y
z

A B C D E F G **H** I J K L M N O P Q R S T U V W X Y Z

hot adjective

1 *The weather will be* **hot** *next week.*

Use **warm** when the weather is quite hot: *It was a lovely* **warm** *spring morning.*

Use **boiling hot**, **baking hot**, and **scorching hot** when it is very hot: *It was a* **baking hot** *summer's day.*

Use **sweltering** when it is too hot: *We couldn't do anything in the afternoon because it was* **sweltering**.
OPPOSITE **cold**

2 *Be careful with that pan—it's* **hot**.

Use **red hot** or **burning hot** for something that is very hot: *The coals on the barbecue were* **red hot**.
OPPOSITE **cold**

3 *Don't spill that* **hot** *water over yourself*

Use **boiling** for a liquid that is hot enough to boil: *You make tea with* **boiling** *water.*

Use **scalding** or **scalding hot** for a liquid that is hot enough to burn your skin: *Don't get into the bath yet—the water's* **scalding hot**.

Use **piping hot** for food or drink that is nice and hot: *She brought us a bowl of* **piping hot** *soup.*
OPPOSITE **cold**

4 *We sat down in front of the* **hot** *fire.*
warm
blazing
roaring
OPPOSITE **cold**

5 *We add chillies to food to make it* **hot**.
spicy
peppery
OPPOSITE **mild**

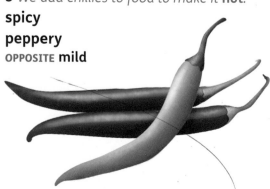

house noun

a home

WORD WEB

Some types of house:

a bungalow
a castle
a cottage

a farmhouse
a mansion
a palace
a villa

hug verb

He **hugged** *his teddy close to him.*
to cuddle
to hold
to embrace

huge adjective

The **huge** *creature came after them.*
great
enormous
gigantic
massive
OPPOSITE **tiny**

hung verb past tense *see* **hang**

hungry adjective

1 *I'm glad it's lunchtime because I'm* **hungry**.

Use **starving**, **famished**, or **ravenous** if you are very hungry: *I was absolutely* **starving** *after swimming.*

Use **peckish** if you are slightly hungry: *It was getting close to lunchtime and I was beginning to feel a bit* **peckish**.

2 *The people have no food, and their children are* **hungry**.

starving
underfed
undernourished

hunt verb

1 *Lions* **hunt** *deer and other animals.*

to chase
to kill

2 *Will you help me* **hunt** *for my purse?*

to look for
to search for

hurry verb

1 *Come on,* **hurry up**!

to be quick *Come on,* **be quick**!
to get a move on *(informal)*

2 *He* **hurried** *out of the room.*

to rush
to dash
to run
to race

hurt verb

1 *You mustn't* **hurt** *animals.*

to injure
to harm

2 *I fell and* **hurt** *my leg.*

to injure
to cut
to graze
to bruise
to sprain
to twist
to dislocate
to break

3 *My head was* **hurting** *after I bumped it.*

to be sore
to be painful

Use **ache** to describe a pain that continues for a long time: *My poor head was* **aching**.

Use **pound** or **throb** to describe a banging pain: *I had a toothache which was* **throbbing** *terribly.*

Use **sting** or **smart** to describe a sharp pain: *The salt water made my eyes* **sting**.

hut noun

We slept in a little **hut** *in the wood.*

a shack
a cabin
a shelter
a shed

A
B
C
D
E
F
G
H
I
J
K
L
M
N
O
P
Q
R
S
T
U
V
W
X
Y
Z

I i

idea noun

1 *I've got an* **idea** *about what you can do during the holidays.*

a suggestion

a plan

a thought

A **brainwave** is a very good idea that you suddenly think of: *We were wondering what to do, then Samir suddenly had a* **brainwave**.

2 *I don't always agree with your* **ideas**.

an opinion

a belief

3 *The film gave us an* **idea** *of what life was like in ancient Rome.*

an impression

a picture

ignore verb

I said hello to them, but they **ignored** *me.*

to take no notice of *They* **took no notice of** *me.*

to pay no attention to *They* **paid no attention to** *me.*

ill adjective

I felt too **ill** *to go to school.*

unwell

poorly

sick

Use **queasy** when you feel as if you are going to be sick: *I was feeling a bit* **queasy** *after eating all that chocolate.*

OPPOSITE **healthy**

illness noun

She is suffering from a nasty **illness**.

Use **ailment** or **complaint** for any illness: *Stomach ache is a very common* **complaint**.

Use **disease** for a serious illness: *Cancer is a very serious* **disease**.

Use **infection** or **bug** for an illness that you catch from other people: *I think I've caught a* **bug** *from someone at school.*

imaginary adjective

1 *Dragons are* **imaginary** *animals.*

mythical

fictional

fictitious

legendary

2 *We played on our* **imaginary** *island.*

pretend

invented

made-up

OPPOSITE **real**

imagine verb

1 *I tried to* **imagine** *what life was like in Roman times.*

to think about

to picture

to visualize

to envisage

2 *It didn't really happen. You only* **imagined** *it.*

to dream

immediately adverb

We need to leave **immediately** *or we'll be late.*

at once
straight away
this minute
instantly

important adjective

1 *There is one* **important** *thing you must remember.*

vital
crucial
essential

2 *The World Cup is a very* **important** *sporting event.*

big
major
special
significant

3 *I was nervous about meeting such an* **important** *person.*

famous
distinguished
prominent
high-ranking
OPPOSITE **unimportant**

impossible adjective

I can't do that—it's **impossible***!*

not possible
not humanly possible
not feasible
OPPOSITE **possible**

improve verb

1 *Your maths is* **improving** *every week.*

to get better
to come on

2 *Try to* **improve** *your handwriting as I can't read it.*

to make progress with

increase verb

1 *Our class has* **increased** *in size.*

to get bigger
to grow
to expand

2 *The noise gradually* **increased***.*

to get louder
to build up

3 *The price of tickets has* **increased** *from five to ten pounds.*

to go up
to rise
to double to become twice as much
OPPOSITE **decrease**

incredible adjective

1 *It seems* **incredible** *that someone could survive for so long in the desert.*

unbelievable
extraordinary
unlikely
unimaginable

2 *This is such an* **incredible** *book that I can't put it down!*

great
excellent
brilliant *(informal)*
wonderful
fantastic
amazing

a
b
c
d
e
f
g
h
i
j
k
l
m
n
o
p
q
r
s
t
u
v
w
x
y
z

information noun
We are collecting **information** about rainforests.

facts
details
data

injure verb
1 He fell and **injured** his leg.

to hurt
to cut
to bruise

Use **graze** when you don't cut yourself very badly: I **grazed** my arm slightly when I fell.

Use **gash** when you cut yourself very badly: He **gashed** his leg on a sharp rock.

2 I landed on my wrist and **injured** it.

to sprain
to twist
to dislocate
to break

injury noun
The captain couldn't play because he had an **injury**.

a wound
a cut
a bruise
a burn
a graze a small cut
a gash a big cut

innocent adjective
The jury decided that he was **innocent** and he was released.

not guilty
blameless
OPPOSITE guilty

insect noun
Henry is fascinated by **insects**.

a bug
a creepy-crawly

WORD WEB
Some **insects**:
an ant
a bee
a beetle
a bluebottle
a bumble bee
a butterfly
a cricket
a daddy-long-legs
a dragonfly
a fly
a grasshopper
a honey bee
a ladybird
a locust
a midge
a mosquito
a moth
a stick insect
a wasp

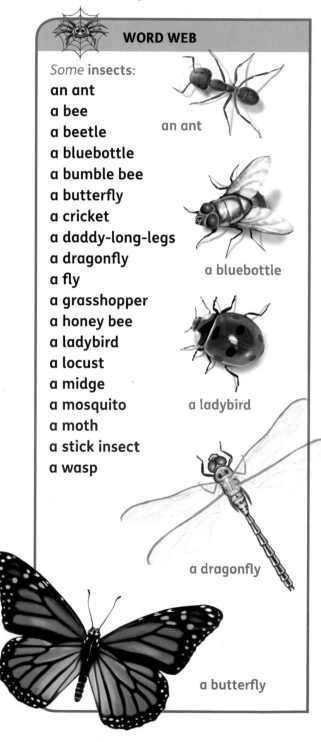

an ant

a bluebottle

a ladybird

a dragonfly

a butterfly

WRITING TIPS

Here are some useful words
for writing about **insects**:

- *The ladybird* **flew** *away.*
- *A wasp was* **buzzing** *around the kitchen.*
- *Bees come together and* **swarm** *when they are looking for a new hive.*
- *A fly* **crawled** *up my leg.*

- *The beetle* **scuttled** *away.*
- *Ants were* **scurrying** *around looking for food.*

a beetle

Insects were swarming all over the earthen mound inside the container.
—Jan Henderson, *Colony*

inspect verb

He **inspected** *the cup to see if it was cracked.*

to examine
to check
to look at

instant adjective

The film was an **instant** *success.*

immediate
instantaneous

instruct verb

1 *The judo teacher* **instructs** *us on how to move safely.*

to coach
to teach
to train

2 *The fire chief* **instructed** *everyone to leave the building.*

to order
to command
to tell

instructions noun

Read the **instructions** *on the packet carefully.*

directions
guidelines

intelligent adjective

He's a very **intelligent** *boy and does well at school.*

clever
bright
brainy *(informal)*
quick
sharp
smart
brilliant
OPPOSITE **stupid**

intend verb

1 *I didn't* **intend** *to upset her.*

to mean
to want
to plan

2 *We* **intend** *to set up a school glee club next year.*

to plan
to propose
to aim

interested adjective

I'm very **interested** *in old coins.*

fascinated *I'm* **fascinated** *by old coins.*

A
B
C
D
E
F
G
H
I
J
K
L
M
N
O
P
Q
R
S
T
U
V
W
X
Y
Z

interesting adjective

*This is a really **interesting** book.*

fascinating
intriguing
exciting
OPPOSITE **boring**

interval noun

*You can have an ice cream during the **interval**.*

a break
an interlude
an intermission

invade verb

*The Romans **invaded** Britain.*

to attack
to occupy
to march into

invent verb

*Who **invented** the first computer?*

to design
to develop
to create
to devise

investigate verb

*For our homework, we had to **investigate** how the Romans lived.*

to explore
to look into
to research
to study

invisible adjective

*Ivy had grown over the old door and made it **invisible**.*

hidden
concealed
OPPOSITE **visible**

invite verb

*I've **invited** all my friends to the party.*

to ask

irritate verb

*My little brother keeps **irritating** me by playing with my toys.*

to annoy
to pester
to bother
to get on someone's nerves (informal)
*My little brother is **getting on my nerves**.*

irritating adjective

*He has some very **irritating** habits.*

annoying
infuriating
maddening

Jj

jail noun
He was locked up in jail.

prison
a cell
a dungeon

jealous adjective
I felt a little bit jealous when I saw her new bike.

envious
resentful

jewel noun
We found a box full of diamonds and other jewels.

a gem
a precious stone

WORD WEB

Some types of **jewel**:	Some types of **jewellery**:
a diamond	a bangle
an emerald	a bracelet
jet	a brooch
an opal	a crown
a pearl	earrings
a ruby	a necklace
a sapphire	a ring
	a tiara

a brooch

rings

job noun
1 *I want to have an interesting job.*

an occupation
a profession
work
a career

2 *I had to do a couple of jobs for my mum.*

a chore
a task

WORD WEB

Some **jobs**:

an architect	an optician
an artist	a photographer
a blacksmith	a pilot
a builder	a plumber
a carpenter	a police officer
a chef	a postal worker
a cook	a professor
a dentist	a reporter
a detective	a sailor
a doctor	a scientist
a dustman	a secretary
an electrician	a shopkeeper
an engineer	a teacher
a farmer	a vet
a firefighter	a waiter
a hairdresser	or **waitress**
a journalist	
a lawyer	
a lecturer	
a librarian	
a mechanic	
a musician	
a nurse	
an office worker	

a police officer

a b c d e f g h i **j** k l m n o p q r s t u v w x y z

A
B
C
D
E
F
G
H
I
J
K
L
M
N
O
P
Q
R
S
T
U
V
W
X
Y
Z

join verb

1 *Join the two wires together.*

to fix

to fasten

to attach

to connect

to tie

to stick

to glue

2 *Why don't you join your local drama group?*

to become a member of

joke noun

1 *He told us some funny jokes.*

a funny story

2 *She hid my school bag as a joke.*

a trick

a prank

journey noun

He set out on his journey.

a trip

An **expedition** is a long journey: *They are planning an expedition to the North Pole.*

A **voyage** is a journey by sea: *The voyage was long and very rough.*

A **flight** is a journey by air: *Our flight took two hours.*

A **drive** is a journey by car: *It's a long drive from London to Inverness.*

A **trek** or **hike** is a long journey on foot: *The trek through the mountains was exhausting.*

jump verb

1 *He jumped into the air and caught the ball.*

to leap

to spring

2 *The cat jumped on the mouse.*

to pounce

to spring

3 *The kangaroo jumped off into the distance.*

to hop

to bound

4 *She was jumping for joy.*

to leap about

to prance about

to skip about

5 *Sammy jumped over the fence.*

to leap over

to vault over

to clear

Use **hurdle** when you jump over something while you are running: *He hurdled the gate.*

Use **clear** when you jump over something easily, without touching it at all: *The horse cleared the last fence in the race.*

6 *She jumped into the water.*

to leap

to dive

to plunge

7 *The sudden noise made me jump.*

to start

to flinch

jungle noun

These animals live deep in the jungle.

a forest

a tropical forest

a rainforest

just adverb

1 *This is just what I wanted.*

exactly

precisely

2 *The classroom is just big enough for all the children.*

hardly

barely

scarcely

keen adjective

1 *All the children are* **keen** *on going to the park.*

enthusiastic about
fond of

2 *She was* **keen** *to go with her sisters.*

eager
anxious

keep verb keeps, keeping, kept

1 *You don't have to give the book back to me. You can* **keep** *it.*

to have
to hold on to

2 **Keep** *still!*

to stay
to remain

3 *They* **keep** *chickens on their farm.*

to have
to look after

4 *I told him to be quiet, but he* **kept** *talking.*

to continue
to carry on

kept verb past tense see keep

kill verb

1 *The knight* **killed** *the mighty dragon.*

to slay

2 *Someone has threatened to* **kill** *him.*

to murder

Use **assassinate** when someone kills a very important person: *Someone has* **assassinated** *the king!*

Use **execute** when people kill someone as a punishment: *In some countries, they* **execute** *criminals instead of sending them to prison.*

3 *The soldiers* **killed** *hundreds of innocent people.*

to slaughter
to massacre

4 *A butcher* **kills** *animals and sells their meat.*

to slaughter

5 *Sometimes a vet has to* **kill** *an animal if it is badly injured.*

to destroy
to put down
to put to sleep

kind adjective

1 *He's a very* **kind** *boy.*

gentle
good-natured
kind-hearted
thoughtful
considerate
unselfish

2 *It was very* **kind** *of you to give so much money to the school.*

generous
OPPOSITE unkind

kind noun

1 *A dictionary is a* **kind** *of book.*

a type
a sort

2 *A terrier is a* **kind** *of dog.*

a breed

3 *A ladybird is a* **kind** *of beetle.*

a species

4 *What* **kind** *of trainers do you want to buy?*

a brand
a make

a b c d e f g h i j **k** l m n o p q r s t u v w x y z

101

A B C D E F G H I J **K** L M N O P Q R S T U V W X Y Z

knew verb past tense *see* **know**

knob noun

1 *He turned the door* **knob**.

a handle

2 *She started fiddling with the* **knobs** *on the machine.*

a switch
a button
a control

knock verb

1 *I* **knocked** *on the door as there was no bell.*

Use **rap** or **tap** when someone knocks not very loudly: *She* **rapped** *lightly on the window.*

Use **bang** or **hammer** when someone knocks loudly: *He* **hammered** *on the door using the brass knocker.*

2 *I fell and* **knocked** *my head against the table.*

to bang
to bump
to hit
to bash

know verb knows, knowing, knew

1 *Do you* **know** *how a car works?*

to understand
to remember

2 *I didn't* **know** *the answer to that question.*

to be sure of
to be certain of *I wasn't* **certain** *of the answer.*

3 *I* **knew** *that someone was watching me.*

to sense
to be aware *I was* **aware** *that someone was watching me.*

4 *As soon as I saw the man, I* **knew** *who he was.*

to recognize
to identify

5 *Do you* **know** *my sister?*

to be acquainted with *Are you* **acquainted** *with my sister?*

Ll

laid verb past tense *see* **lay**

land noun

1 *This is good* **land** *for growing crops.*
ground
earth
soil
2 *He has travelled to many faraway* **lands** *in the story.*
a country
a nation
a region
a kingdom a land with a king or queen

land verb

1 *The plane should* **land** *at seven o'clock.*
to touch down
to come down
to arrive
2 *They rowed towards the island and* **landed** *on a small beach.*
to come ashore
to go ashore
3 *The bird* **landed** *on a small branch.*
to alight
to fly down onto
to come to rest on

large adjective

1 *He was carrying a* **large**, *heavy box.*
big
Use **huge** or **enormous** for something that is very large: *He came out with the most* **enormous** *sandwich I had ever seen.*

Use **massive** or **gigantic** for something that is very large indeed: *Some dinosaurs were so* **massive** *that they couldn't run very fast.*

2 *There are* **large** *buildings in the city centre.*
big
tall
Use **spacious** for buildings that have plenty of space inside: *Our new flat is bright and* **spacious**.

Use **grand** or **magnificent** for things that are very large and beautiful: *The prince lived in a* **magnificent** *palace.*

3 *She gave me a* **large** *portion of chips.*
big
generous
sizeable
OPPOSITE **small**

last adjective

Z is the **last** *letter of the alphabet.*
final
OPPOSITE **first**

last verb

The party **lasted** *for two hours.*
to continue
to go on

late adjective

We missed the concert as the bus was **late**.
delayed
overdue
OPPOSITE **early**

A B C D E F G H I J K **L** M N O P Q R S T U V W X Y Z

laugh verb

*All the children started **laughing**.*

Use **chuckle** when someone laughs quietly to themselves: *The professor read the letter and **chuckled** to himself.*

Use **giggle**, **titter**, or **snigger** when someone laughs in a slightly silly way: *The girls **giggled** as he walked past.*

Use **cackle** when someone laughs in a nasty way: *The old witch **cackled** with laughter.*

Use **guffaw**, **roar with laughter**, or **shriek with laughter** when someone laughs very loudly: *He threw back his head and **guffawed** loudly.*

Use **burst out laughing** when someone suddenly starts to laugh: *We all **burst out laughing** when we saw his new hat.*

law noun

*Everyone must obey the **laws** of the country.*

a rule
a regulation

lay verb lays, laying, laid

*I **laid** the clothes on my bed so I could decide what to wear.*

to put
to place
to spread

layer noun

1 *There was a thick **layer** of dust on the old books.*

a coating
a covering
a film

2 *The pond was covered in a **layer** of ice.*

a sheet

lead verb leads, leading, led

1 *He **led** us to the secret cave.*

to take
to guide

2 *Who is going to **lead** the expedition?*

to command
to be in charge of

3 *Our team was **leading** at the end of the first round.*

to be winning
to be in the lead *Our team was **in the lead**.*

leak verb

*Water was **leaking** out of the pipe.*

to drip
to trickle
to seep
to spill

lean verb leans, leaning, leaned or leant

1 *She **leaned** forward to look out of the window.*

to stretch
to bend

2 *The old building **leans** to one side.*

to slant
to tilt

3 *He was **leaning** against the wall.*

to recline

4 *He **leaned** his bicycle against the wall.*

to prop
to rest

leant verb past tense see **lean**

leap verb leaps, leaping, leaped or leapt

1 *The cat **leaped** into the air.*

to jump
to spring

2 *She **leaped** over the fence.*
to hurdle *She **hurdled** the fence.*
to clear *She **cleared** the fence.*
3 *She **leaped** into the water.*
to jump
to dive
to plunge

learn verb **learns, learning, learned** or **learnt**
*We are **learning** about the Vikings at school.*
to find out
to discover

learnt verb past tense *see* **learn**

leave verb **leaves, leaving, left**
1 *What time does the train **leave**?*
to go
to set off
to depart
OPPOSITE **arrive**
2 *The ship **leaves** at nine o'clock.*
to sail
to depart
3 *The plane **leaves** at 11.30 p.m.*
to take off
to depart
4 *She **left** the party when no one was looking.*
to sneak off
to slip away
to creep off
5 *He **left** the room in a terrible temper.*
to go off
to storm off
6 *Where did you **leave** your bag?*
to put
7 *All my friends went and **left** me alone!*
to desert
to abandon

led verb past tense *see* **lead**

left verb past tense *see* **leave**

let verb **lets, letting, let**
*Will you **let** me ride your bike?*
to allow *Will you **allow** me to ride your bike?*
to give someone permission *Will you give me **permission** to ride your bike?*

level adjective
1 *You need a nice **level** surface to put your laptop on.*
flat
even
smooth
horizontal
OPPOSITE **uneven**
2 *Their scores were **level** at half time.*
even
equal
the same
OPPOSITE **different**

lie noun
*Don't tell **lies** as someone will find you out.*
a fib (informal)
an untruth

lie verb
1 *She was **lying** on the sofa.*
to rest
to lounge
to recline
to sprawl
to stretch out
2 *I don't believe him—I think he's **lying**.*
to fib
to tell lies
to bluff

a
b
c
d
e
f
g
h
i
j
k
l
m
n
o
p
q
r
s
t
u
v
w
x
y
z

A
B
C
D
E
F
G
H
I
J
K
L
M
N
O
P
Q
R
S
T
U
V
W
X
Y
Z

lift noun

1 *We took the **lift** up to the fifth floor.*
an elevator
2 *He gave us a **lift** in his new car.*
a ride

lift verb

*Ben **lifted** the trophy into the air proudly.*
to raise
to hoist
to pick up

light adjective

1 *My suitcase is quite **light**.*
not very heavy
OPPOSITE **heavy**
2 *Our classroom is nice and **light**.*
bright
well-lit
OPPOSITE **dim**
3 *She was wearing **light** blue leggings*
pale
pastel
OPPOSITE **dark**

light noun

1 *I couldn't see very well because there wasn't much **light**.*
daylight
sunlight
moonlight
brightness
2 *Please could you switch the **light** on?*
an electric light
a lamp

WORD WEB

*Some types of **light**:*
floodlights lights at a sports ground
a headlight a light on a car
a lamp
a searchlight a powerful torch
a spotlight a light on a stage
a street light
a torch

WRITING TIPS

Here are some useful words for writing about **light**:
- *I could see a light **shining** somewhere in the forest.*
- *A pale light **glowed** beneath the water.*
- *The fairy lights **gleamed** and **glimmered** in the darkness.*
- *The water **glistened** and **sparkled** in the sunlight.*
- *Stars **twinkled** above us.*
- *The light from the lighthouse **flashed** on and off.*
- *The searchlights **flickered** brightly.*
- *The headlights **glared** in the darkness.*

like preposition

*Your pencil case is **like** mine.*

the same as
similar to

like verb

1 *I **like** our new teacher.*

to get on well with
to be fond of

Use **love**, **adore**, or **idolize** if you like someone a lot: *She **idolizes** her grandad!*

2 *Ben **likes** playing chess.*

to be keen on
to enjoy

Use **love**, **adore**, or **be mad about** if you like something a lot: *She **is mad about** ponies!*

3 *I think that boy **likes** you!*

to fancy
OPPOSITE **dislike**

likely adjective

*It's quite **likely** that it will rain later.*

possible
probable
OPPOSITE **unlikely**

line noun

1 *Draw a **line** across the top of the page.*

a mark

2 *Her old face was covered in **lines**.*

wrinkles

3 *We all stood in a **line**.*

a row
a queue

litter noun

*The playground was covered in **litter**.*

rubbish
mess

little adjective

OVERUSED WORD

Here are some more interesting words for **little**:

1 *They live in a **little** house on the edge of the village.*

small

Use **tiny** or **titchy** for something that is very small: *The mouse began to dig with its **tiny** paws.*

Use **cramped** or **poky** for a house or room that is too small: *They lived in a **cramped** one-room flat.*

2 *He's only a **little** boy.*

young

3 *It's only a **little** problem.*

small
slight
minor

4 *We had a **little** chat.*

short
brief
OPPOSITE **big**

live verb

1 *Plants cannot **live** without water.*

to exist
to survive
to remain alive

2 *We **live** in London.*

to reside

lively adjective

*The puppies were **lively** and lots of fun.*

active
busy
energetic

boisterous
playful
OPPOSITE **quiet**

load verb

1 *We loaded the suitcases into the car.*
to put
to lift
2 *We loaded the trolley with food.*
to fill
to pack
to pile up

lock noun

We need to put a lock on the shed door.
a bolt
a padlock

lock verb

Don't forget to lock the door.
to shut
to fasten
to bolt
to secure

lonely adjective

1 *I felt lonely when all my friends had left.*
alone
isolated
friendless
forlorn
2 *They live in a lonely part of the country.*

Use **remote** or **isolated** for a place that is far away from towns and cities: *On top of the hill is an isolated farmhouse.*

Use **secluded** for a place that people cannot see: *Behind the house is a secluded garden.*

Use **uninhabited** for a place where no one lives: *The northern side of the island is uninhabited.*

long adjective

1 *It's quite a long movie and is very boring.*
lengthy
2 *We had to sit and listen to his long speech.*
endless
interminable
long-drawn-out
OPPOSITE **short**

look verb

OVERUSED WORD

Here are some more interesting words for **look**:

1 *I'm looking at a squirrel in the garden.*
to watch
to observe
to study
2 *She looked at the picture.*

Use **glance** or **peep** when you look at something quickly: *I glanced at the clock to see what time it was.*

Use **stare** or **gaze** when you look at something for a long time: *We gazed at the beautiful view.*

Use **peer** or **squint** when you look at something carefully because you cannot see it very well: *We peered through the window into the dark room.*

3 *I could see that Lucy was looking at me.*

Use **stare** if you look at someone for a long time: *Why are you staring at me?*

Use **glare**, **glower**, or **scowl** if you look at someone angrily: *Mum glared at me angrily.*

4 *That dog doesn't look very friendly.*
to seem
to appear

A B C D E F G H I J K **L** M N O P Q R S T U V W X Y Z

look for

*I'll help you **look for** your gloves.*

to search for
to hunt for
to try to find

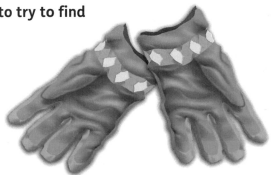

loose adjective

1 *One of my teeth is **loose** and I wonder how long it will be before it falls out.*

wobbly
shaky
OPPOSITE **secure**

2 *The rope was a bit **loose** and didn't feel safe.*

slack
OPPOSITE **tight**

3 *I like to wear **loose** clothes.*

baggy
big
oversized
OPPOSITE **tight**

lose verb loses, losing, lost

1 *I've **lost** my earphones somewhere in the house.*

to mislay
to misplace
OPPOSITE **find**

2 *Our team **lost** the game.*

to be defeated
OPPOSITE **win**

lost verb past tense *see* lose

loud adjective

1 *We heard a **loud** bang.*

noisy
deafening
ear-splitting

2 *I don't like **loud** music.*

blaring

3 *He spoke in a **loud** voice.*

Use **booming** or **thunderous** for a deep voice: *'Come here!' he shouted in a **booming** voice.*

Use **shrill** or **piercing** for a high voice: *'Get away from me,' he shrieked in a **shrill** voice.*
OPPOSITE **quiet**

love verb

1 *Alice **loves** her brother.*

to be very fond of
to adore

Use **worship** or **idolize** if you love someone and admire them a lot: *He **idolizes** his elder brother who is very good at sport!*

2 *Ben **loves** sport!*

to enjoy
to be very keen on
to be obsessed with
to be mad about
OPPOSITE **hate**

a
b
c
d
e
f
g
h
i
j
k
l
m
n
o
p
q
r
s
t
u
v
w
x
y
z

109

A B C D E F G H I J K **L** M N O P Q R S T U V W X Y Z

lovely adjective

OVERUSED WORD

Here are some more interesting words for **lovely**:

1 *What a* **lovely** *picture!*

beautiful
gorgeous
delightful

2 *You look* **lovely** *today.*

pretty
beautiful
attractive

Use **gorgeous** or **stunning** if someone is very lovely: *She looks absolutely* **stunning** *in that dress!*

Use **glamorous** if someone looks lovely and rich: *The stars all looked very* **glamorous** *in their evening dresses.*

3 *The food was* **lovely**.

delicious
tasty

4 *These flowers smell* **lovely**.

beautiful
fragrant
perfumed

5 *He's a* **lovely** *boy.*

kind
pleasant
charming
polite

6 *It was a* **lovely** *day for sports day.*

beautiful
warm
sunny
glorious
wonderful

7 *We had a* **lovely** *time on holiday.*

enjoyable
wonderful
fantastic

OPPOSITE **horrible**

low adjective

1 *We sat on a* **low** *bench under the tree.*

small

2 *Their prices are usually quite* **low** *so we can afford to shop there.*

reasonable
reduced

3 *He spoke in a* **low** *voice and no one could hear him.*

soft
deep

OPPOSITE **high**

luck noun

It was just by **luck** *that Alice phoned me when she did.*

chance
accident
coincidence

lucky adjective

We were **lucky** *that we got home before the rain started.*

fortunate

OPPOSITE **unlucky**

luggage noun

*We put all our **luggage** on the train.*

bags

suitcases

baggage

lump noun

1 *She gave him some bread and a **lump** of cheese.*

a piece

a chunk

a block

a wedge

2 *I've got a **lump** on my head where I hit it.*

a bump

a swelling

a
b
c
d
e
f
g
h
i
j
k
l
m
n
o
p
q
r
s
t
u
v
w
x
y
z

111

A
B
C
D
E
F
G
H
I
J
K
L
M
N
O
P
Q
R
S
T
U
V
W
X
Y
Z

Mm

made verb past tense *see* **make**

magic noun

1 *He says he can use **magic** to make rain fall from the sky.*

sorcery
witchcraft
wizardry

2 *The conjuror performed some **magic** and we were dazzled by the tricks.*

conjuring
tricks

magician noun

1 *He was taken prisoner by an evil **magician**.*

a wizard
a sorcerer
an enchanter

2 *The children watched the **magician** doing magic tricks.*

a conjuror

magnificent adjective

*The king lived in a **magnificent** palace.*

grand
splendid
wonderful

main adjective

*The **main** ingredient of bread is flour.*

most important
principal
chief
essential

make verb makes, making, made

1 *We managed to **make** a shelter out of some old pieces of wood.*

to build
to form
to construct
to create
to put together

2 *They **make** cars in that factory.*

to produce
to manufacture
to assemble

3 *The heat of the sun can be used to **make** electricity.*

to generate
to produce
to create

4 *We **made** some cakes and biscuits for the party.*

to bake
to cook
to prepare

5 *You can **make** this old dish into a bird bath.*

to change
to turn
to transform

6 *Please don't **make** too much mess.*

to create
to cause

7 *They **made** me clean the floor although I didn't have time.*

to force
to order *They **ordered** me to clean the floor.*

man noun

*I'll ask the **man** in the ticket office.*

a gentleman
a bloke *(informal)*
a guy *(informal)*

a **chap** (informal)
a **bachelor** an unmarried man
a **husband** a married man
a **father** a man who has children
a **widower** a man whose wife has died

manage verb

1 *I finally* **managed** *to open the door.*
to succeed in *I finally* **succeeded in** *opening the door.*
2 *His father* **manages** *a shop.*
to run
to be in charge of

map noun

He drew a **map** *to show us how to get to the school.*
a plan
a diagram

mark noun

1 *His hands left dirty* **marks** *all over the bathroom towels.*
a stain
a spot
a smear
a smudge
a streak
2 *He had a red* **mark** *on his face.*
footprints *His feet had left deep* **footprints** *in the snow.*
tracks

market noun

You can buy all sorts of interesting things at the **market**.
a bazaar
a street market
a car boot sale

marvellous adjective

We had a **marvellous** *holiday and were sad to come home.*
wonderful
brilliant
great
fantastic
perfect

mass noun

1 *There was a* **mass** *of rubbish to clear away.*
a heap
a pile
a mound
a stack
2 *There was a* **mass** *of people in front of the stage.*
a group
a crowd
a horde

massive adjective

They live in a **massive** *house with seven bedrooms.*
enormous
huge
gigantic
colossal
immense
OPPOSITE **tiny**

match noun

1 *We watched a football* **match** *on TV.*
a game
2 *We went to see a boxing* **match** *at the local gym.*
a contest
a fight

a
b
c
d
e
f
g
h
i
j
k
l
m
n
o
p
q
r
s
t
u
v
w
x
y
z

A
B
C
D
E
F
G
H
I
J
K
L
M
N
O
P
Q
R
S
T
U
V
W
X
Y
Z

material noun

1 *Stone is a good building* **material**.

a substance

2 *Her skirt was made of bright yellow* **material**.

cloth
fabric

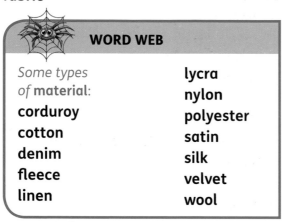

WORD WEB

Some types of **material**:

corduroy	**lycra**
cotton	**nylon**
denim	**polyester**
fleece	**satin**
linen	**silk**
	velvet
	wool

maybe adverb

Maybe *they'll come later.*

perhaps
possibly
OPPOSITE **definitely**

meal noun

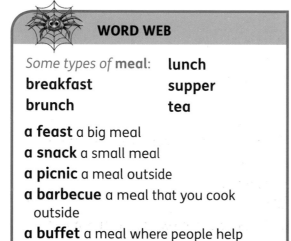

WORD WEB

Some types of **meal**:

breakfast	**lunch**
brunch	**supper**
	tea

a feast a big meal
a snack a small meal
a picnic a meal outside
a barbecue a meal that you cook outside
a buffet a meal where people help themselves to food

mean adjective

1 *That was a really* **mean** *thing to do and it hurt my feelings.*

unkind
nasty
selfish
cruel
vindictive
OPPOSITE **kind**

2 *He's really* **mean** *with his money and tries not to spend anything.*

stingy
tight-fisted
miserly
OPPOSITE **generous**

mean verb means, meaning, meant

We **meant** *to be home by six.*

to intend
to aim
to plan

meant verb past tense see mean

measurement noun

We wrote down the **measurements** *of the room.*

the size
the dimensions
the length
the width
the breadth
the height
the depth

medium adjective

I am **medium** *height for my age.*

average
normal
ordinary

meet verb meets, meeting, met

1 *We'll* **meet** *at the swimming pool at 11 a.m. for the 11.15 a.m. class.*

to meet up
to get together

2 *Sarah will* **meet** *us at the shops later.*

to join
to see

3 *As I was walking along the lane, I* **met** *my friend Alice.*

to encounter
to see
to bump into

4 *I haven't* **met** *our new neighbours yet and they lived there for over a month now.*

to get to know
to be introduced to *I haven't* **been introduced** *to them yet.*

5 *Two rivers* **meet** *here.*

to join
to come together
to merge
to converge

meeting noun

The teachers are having a **meeting** *in the staff room.*

a gathering
a discussion
a conference
a get-together

melt verb

The ice **melted** *in the heat of the sun.*

to thaw
to soften
to unfreeze

mend verb

1 *Do you think you can* **mend** *my CD player?*

to repair
to fix

2 *Dad likes* **mending** *old furniture.*

to do up
to restore
to renovate

3 *I need to* **mend** *these jeans.*

to sew up
to patch

mention verb

1 *Nobody* **mentioned** *the stolen money.*

to talk about
to refer to
to allude to

2 *She* **mentioned** *that the house looked very untidy.*

to say
to remark

merry adjective

They clapped their hands and sang a **merry** *song.*

happy
cheerful
joyful
jolly
OPPOSITE **sad**

mess noun

1 *Who's going to clear up all this* **mess**?

clutter
untidiness
litter

2 *The papers were all in a terrible* **mess**.

a muddle
a jumble

a b c d e f g h i j k l m n o p q r s t u v w x y z

A
B
C
D
E
F
G
H
I
J
K
L
M
N
O
P
Q
R
S
T
U
V
W
X
Y
Z

message noun

*She sent me a **message** to say that she was ill.*

a letter
a note
an email
a text message

messy adjective

*The room was very **messy** and we only had an hour to tidy up.*

untidy
cluttered
dirty
disorganized
OPPOSITE **neat**

met verb past tense *see* meet

middle noun

1 *There was a big puddle in the **middle** of the playground.*

the centre

2 *They live right in the **middle** of London.*

the centre
the heart

3 *Is it possible to dig right through to the **middle** of the earth?*

the core
the centre

mild adjective

1 *The soup had a **mild** flavour.*

delicate
subtle
bland

2 *It was only a **mild** illness.*

slight

3 *The weather was quite **mild**.*

warm
calm
pleasant
balmy

mind noun

*I don't know how he keeps all those facts in his **mind**.*

brain
head
memory

mind verb

*I don't **mind** if you're a bit late.*

to object
to care
to be bothered

miserable adjective

*I felt really **miserable** when my friends left.*

sad
unhappy
depressed
gloomy
wretched
OPPOSITE **cheerful**

miss verb

1 *I just managed to **miss** hitting the window with the ball.*

to avoid

2 *I tried to catch the ball, but I **missed** it.*

to drop

3 *Hurry, or you'll **miss** the bus.*

to be late for

4 *I really **missed** my brother when he was away.*

to long for
to pine for

missing adjective

*My phone is **missing**.*

lost

nowhere to be found *The phone was nowhere to be found.*

mist noun

*They got lost in the **mist**.*

fog

haze

mistake noun

1 *I knew I had made a **mistake**.*

an error

A **blunder** is a bad mistake. *John knew that he had made a terrible **blunder**.*

A **slip-up** is a small mistake. *She knew that if she made even one little **slip-up** she would be caught.*

An **oversight** is a mistake you make when you forget to do something. *My name was missed off the list because of an **oversight**.*

2 *There must be a **mistake** in your calculations.*

an error

an inaccuracy

3 *The teacher corrected all the **mistakes** in my story.*

a spelling mistake

a misspelling

mix verb

1 Mix *red and yellow paint together to make orange.*

to blend

to combine

2 Mix *all the ingredients together in a bowl.*

to stir

to blend

to beat

to whisk

mixture noun

1 *She dipped her finger into the cake **mixture**.*

a mix

2 *We made up a **mixture** of blue and yellow paint.*

a blend

a combination

3 *We had pizza with a **mixture** of different vegetables.*

a variety

an assortment

moan verb

1 *He **moaned** with pain.*

to groan

to wail

2 *I wish you would stop **moaning** about everything!*

to complain

to grumble

to whinge

modern adjective

1 *She likes to wear very **modern** clothes.*

fashionable

trendy

stylish

a
b
c
d
e
f
g
h
i
j
k
l
m
n
o
p
q
r
s
t
u
v
w
x
y
z

A B C D E F G H I J K L **M** N O P Q R S T U V W X Y Z

2 *The factory is full of very* **modern** *machinery.*

new
up-to-date
futuristic
OPPOSITE **old-fashioned**

modest adjective

1 *She was very* **modest** *about all her achievements.*

humble
self-effacing
OPPOSITE **conceited**

2 *He was too* **modest** *to wear fancy dress to the party.*

shy
bashful
coy

moment noun

Could you just wait a **moment**?

a minute
a second
an instant

money noun

1 *I have saved* **money** *to buy a new iPod.*

cash
change
coins
silver
coppers
notes
currency

2 *Some pop stars have got plenty of* **money** *and buy houses and cars.*

wealth
riches

3 *He earns* **money** *by working in a hospital.*

wages
a salary
an income
pay

4 *My parents give me* **money** *every week.*

pocket money
an allowance

5 *Have you got any* **money** *in the bank?*

savings
funds

monster noun

A huge **monster** *was coming towards them.*

a beast
a creature

WRITING TIPS

Here are some useful words for writing about **monsters**:

* *The* **huge**, **ugly** *giant was coming towards us.*
* *The ogre was* **hideous**, *with a* **horrible**, **hairy** *face.*
* *In the cave lived a* **fierce** *and* **terrible** **dragon**.
* *The* **terrifying** *dragon was huge, with green* **scaly** *skin.*
* *We had heard stories of a* **fearsome** *werewolf that lived in the forest.*

Griswold Gristle and Judge Cedric were stumbling through the wood, running as if all the monsters in the world were after them. —Ian Ogilvy, *Measle and the Slitherghoul*

WORD WEB

Some types of monster:
a dragon
a giant
an ogre
a troll
a vampire
a werewolf

moody adjective

*Why are you so **moody** with everyone today?*

bad-tempered
sulky
grumpy
irritable
sullen

OPPOSITE **cheerful**

more adjective

*We need some **more** money.*

extra
additional

mountain noun

*We could see the **mountains** in the distance.*

a hill
a peak
a volcano
a mountain range a group of mountains

move verb

OVERUSED WORD

Here are some more interesting words for **move**:

1 *We **moved** the table into the other room.*

to push
to pull
to carry

Use **drag** when something is very heavy: *They **dragged** the heavy crate outside.*

2 *The train **moved** out of the station.*

Use **to speed**, **to race**, **to hurtle**, **to whizz**, or **to zoom** when something moves very quickly: *A sports car **zoomed** past us.*

Use **to crawl**, **to creep**, or **to trundle** when something moves very slowly: *The train **crawled** along at 25 miles per hour.*

Use **to glide**, **to slide**, **to float**, or **to drift** when something moves smoothly and gracefully: *The little boat **drifted** slowly through the water.*

Use **to advance** or **to proceed** when something moves forwards: *Let us **proceed** to the castle.*

Use **to retreat**, **to draw back**, or **to withdraw** when something moves backwards: *The army was losing the battle and had to **retreat**.*

Use **to rise**, **to climb**, or **to ascend** when something moves upwards: *The rocket **ascended** into space.*

Use **to fall**, **to descend**, **to drop**, or **to sink** when something moves downwards: *The hot-air balloon **sank** gently down to the ground.*

Use **to stir**, **to sway**, **to wave**, **to flap**, or **to shake** when something moves about: *The huge trees **swayed** gently in the breeze.*

Use **to spin**, **to turn**, **to rotate**, **to revolve**, **to twirl**, or **to whirl** when something moves round and round: *The dancers **whirled** round and round.*

3 *He sat in the corner and refused to **move**.*

to budge
to shift
to change places

A B C D E F G H I J K L **M** N O P Q R S T U V W X Y Z

mud noun
*His boots were covered in **mud**.*

dirt
muck
clay
sludge

muddle noun
*My school books were in a terrible **muddle**.*

a mess
a jumble

music noun

mysterious adjective
*She disappeared in a very **mysterious** way.*

strange
weird
puzzling
baffling
mystifying

mystery noun
*The police solved the **mystery** of the crime.*

a puzzle
a riddle
a secret

WORD WEB

Some types of music:
blues
classical
country
folk
jazz
opera
pop
rap
reggae
rock

Some types of musician:
a composer
a performer
a player
a singer

Some stringed instruments:
a banjo
a cello
a double bass
a guitar
a harp
a mandolin
a sitar
a ukulele
a viola
a violin

Some woodwind instruments:
a bassoon
a clarinet
a flute
an oboe
a piccolo
a recorder

Some brass instruments:
a bugle
a cornet
a horn
a saxophone
a trombone
a trumpet
a tuba

Some keyboard instruments:
an accordion
a harpsichord
a keyboard
an organ
a piano

Some percussion instruments:
cymbals
a drum
a glockenspiel
a tambourine
a triangle
a xylophone

Nn

name noun

What is your name?

a first name
a surname
a family name
a nickname

nasty adjective

1 *I don't like the nasty way that person speaks to people.*

horrible
unpleasant
mean
spiteful
unkind
obnoxious
horrid
malevolent

2 *There was a nasty smell in the kitchen and it made me feel ill.*

horrible
unpleasant
revolting
disgusting
foul
repellent

3 *She's got a nasty cut on her arm.*

bad
awful
terrible
painful
OPPOSITE nice

natural adjective

1 *My favourite jumper is made of natural wool.*

real
genuine
pure
OPPOSITE artificial

2 *It's natural to be upset when your pet dies.*

normal
ordinary
usual
OPPOSITE unnatural

naughty adjective

Have you ever been naughty?

bad
badly behaved
disobedient
mischievous
disruptive
bad-mannered
rude
OPPOSITE well behaved

near adjective

Our house is near the school.

close to
next to
beside

nearly adverb

I've nearly finished.

almost
virtually
just about
practically

a
b
c
d
e
f
g
h
i
j
k
l
m
n
o
p
q
r
s
t
u
v
w
x
y
z

121

A
B
C
D
E
F
G
H
I
J
K
L
M
N
O
P
Q
R
S
T
U
V
W
X
Y
Z

neat adjective

1 *Her bedroom is always very* **neat.**

tidy

clean

orderly

spick and span

2 *He looked very* **neat** *in his new uniform.*

smart

elegant

well turned out

OPPOSITE **untidy**

necessary adjective

It is **necessary** *to water plants in dry weather.*

important

essential

vital

OPPOSITE **unnecessary**

need verb

1 *All plants and animals* **need** *water.*

to require

to depend on

to rely on

to want

2 *You* **need** *to finish your homework.*

to have to *You* **have to** *finish your homework.*

should *You* **should** *finish your homework.*

nervous adjective

1 *Are you* **nervous** *about starting school?*

worried

anxious

apprehensive

2 *The horses seemed very* **nervous.**

jumpy

agitated

fearful

panicky

tense

OPPOSITE **calm**

new adjective

1 *She was wearing a* **new** *dress.*

brand new

2 *The hospital has lots of* **new** *equipment.*

modern

up-to-date

state-of-the-art

3 *See if you can think of some* **new** *ideas.*

fresh

different

novel

innovative

OPPOSITE **old**

next adjective

1 *They live in the* **next** *street.*

nearest

closest

adjacent

2 *They set off the* **next** *day.*

following

nice adjective

OVERUSED WORD

Here are some more interesting words for **nice**:

1 *You look very **nice** with your hair short.*

Use **pretty**, **beautiful**, or **lovely** to describe a woman or girl. Use **handsome** to describe a boy or man. Use **gorgeous** or **stunning** for someone who looks very nice: *You look absolutely **stunning** in that dress.*

Use **glamorous** for someone who looks very rich: *All the pop stars were arriving for the ceremony looking very **glamorous**.*

2 *She likes wearing **nice** clothes.*

pretty
lovely
beautiful
smart
elegant

Use **fashionable** or **stylish** for clothes that look modern: *I saw a pair of really **stylish** shoes that I want to buy.*

3 *The food was very **nice**.*

delicious
tasty
mouth-watering

4 *Some of the flowers smell very **nice**.*

pleasant
fragrant
perfumed

5 *Did you have a **nice** holiday?*

pleasant
lovely
enjoyable
wonderful
fantastic

6 *He's a very **nice** boy.*

friendly
kind
likeable
pleasant

Use **helpful** or **thoughtful** for someone who thinks about other people or helps other people: *It was very **thoughtful** of you to unpack the shopping for me.*

Use **charming** or **polite** for someone who behaves well and isn't rude to people: *Remember to be **polite** to your aunt and uncle.*

7 *I hope we have **nice** weather for our trip to the beach.*

fine
lovely
pleasant
beautiful
warm
sunny

Use **glorious** or **wonderful** for weather that is very nice: *It was a **glorious**, hot summer's day.*

OPPOSITE **horrible**

noise noun

1 *The* **noise** *of the engines was deafening.*

din

racket

row

rumpus

uproar

2 *I heard a sudden* **noise***.*

a sound

a bang

a clang

a clank

a scream

a shout

A **clatter** is the sound of things banging against each other: *The plates fell to the floor with a* **clatter***.*

A **thud** or **thump** is the sound of something heavy falling to the floor: *The book fell to the floor with a* **thud***.*

A **roar** or **rumble** is a long, low sound: *We heard a* **rumble** *of thunder in the distance.*

A **screech** is a loud, screaming sound: *The brakes* **screeched** *loudly when the racing cars went round the sharp bends.*

A **squeak** is a very high sound: *The gate opened with a* **squeak***.*

noisy adjective

1 *The engines were so* **noisy** *that we couldn't hear ourselves speak.*

loud

deafening

ear-splitting

2 *She asked the children not to be so* **noisy** *as she was trying to sleep.*

loud

rowdy

boisterous

OPPOSITE **quiet**

normal adjective

1 *It's quite **normal** to feel tired at the end of the day.*

natural

common

usual

2 *It looked like a **normal** car but she'd been told that it was very expensive.*

ordinary

standard

typical

average

everyday

OPPOSITE **abnormal**

nosy adjective

*Don't be so **nosy**!*

Use **inquisitive** or **curious** when someone wants to know about something: *I was **curious** to know why Oscar wasn't at school.*

Use **snooping** or **prying** when someone wants to know too much about something: *I wish those **snooping** kids would mind their own business!*

notice noun

*We put up a **notice** to tell people about our play.*

a poster

a sign

an announcement

an advertisement

notice verb

*I **noticed** that there were no lights on in the house.*

to observe

to see

to spot

nuisance noun

*The rain was a **nuisance**.*

a problem

a pain

an inconvenience

a pest

Use **inconvenience** for something that causes you a lot of problems: *It can be a terrible **inconvenience** not having a car.*

Use **pest** for a person or animal that annoys you: *My little sister is such a **pest**!*

A
B
C
D
E
F
G
H
I
J
K
L
M
N
O
P
Q
R
S
T
U
V
W
X
Y
Z

Oo

obey verb

You must obey the rules.

to abide by *You must abide by the rules.*
to not break *You must not break the rules.*
OPPOSITE **disobey**

obvious adjective

It was obvious that he was lying.

clear
plain
apparent
evident

occasionally adverb

We occasionally go swimming.

sometimes
from time to time
now and then

odd adjective

It seemed odd that the school was so quiet.

strange
funny
peculiar
curious
weird
OPPOSITE **normal**

offer verb

1 *She offered me a piece of cake with my tea.*
to give
to hand
2 *Tom offered to wash up after dinner.*
to volunteer

often adverb

We often go swimming on Saturdays.
frequently
regularly
Use **again and again** or **time after time** for something that happens a number of times: *I tried again and again, but I couldn't open the door.*

old adjective

OVERUSED WORD

Here are some more interesting words for **old**:

1 *My grandmother is quite old.*
elderly
aged
OPPOSITE **young**

2 *Can we get a new TV? This one is old!*
Use **ancient** for something that is very old: *I found some ancient maps in the attic.*

Use **old-fashioned** or **out-of-date** for something that isn't very modern: *There was an old-fashioned radio in the kitchen.*
OPPOSITE **new**

3 *My dad collects old coins.*
ancient
Use **antique** for something that is old and valuable: *My aunt told me off for putting a cup on her antique table.*
OPPOSITE **modern**

4 *He was wearing some old jeans.*
tatty
shabby
scruffy
worn-out
OPPOSITE **new**

open adjective

*Someone had left the door **open**.*

ajar
wide open
unlocked
unfastened
gaping
OPPOSITE **closed**

open verb

1 *He opened the door.*

to unlock
to push open

Use **fling open** or **throw open** when you open something suddenly or roughly: *Jack flung open the door to the attic and cried, 'Go and see for yourselves!'*

Use **break down** when you open a door by breaking it: *The police had to break down the door to get into the house.*

2 *The door opened.*

to swing open

Use **burst open** or **fly open** when something opens suddenly or quickly: *Suddenly, the door burst open and the teacher marched in looking very angry.*

OPPOSITE **close**

opening noun

*We crawled through a tiny **opening** in the wooden fence.*

a gap
a hole
a space
a crack

opposite adjective

1 *My friend lives on the **opposite** side of the road to me.*

facing

2 *North is the **opposite** direction to south.*

different
opposing

order noun

*You must obey my **orders** or things could go wrong.*

a command
an instruction

order verb

1 *He ordered us to stand still.*

to tell
to command
to instruct

2 *We ordered some sandwiches and drinks.*

to ask for
to request
to send for

a
b
c
d
e
f
g
h
i
j
k
l
m
n
o
p
q
r
s
t
u
v
w
x
y
z

A
B
C
D
E
F
G
H
I
J
K
L
M
N
O
P
Q
R
S
T
U
V
W
X
Y
Z

ordinary adjective

1 *It was just an **ordinary** day but we had a great time.*
normal
usual
typical
everyday
routine
unexciting

2 *It's just an **ordinary** house.*
normal
standard
average
OPPOSITE **special**

organize verb

*Our teacher **organized** a trip to the zoo.*
to arrange
to plan
to set up

original adjective

1 *Try to think of some **original** ideas for your stories.*
new
fresh
imaginative

2 *The **original** version has been lost.*
first
earliest
initial

outing noun

*We went on an **outing** to the country park.*
a trip
an excursion
an expedition

own verb

*Do you **own** a bike?*
to have
to possess

own up

*He **owned up** to stealing the money.*
to admit *He **admitted** stealing the money.*
to confess *He **confessed** to stealing the money.*

Pp

paid verb past tense *see* **pay**

pain noun

1 *I've got a* **pain** *in my stomach and I feel sick.*

Use **ache** for a pain that continues for a long time: *I could still feel an* **ache** *in my leg where the horse had kicked me.*

Use **twinge** or **pang** for a sudden sharp pain: *I felt a sudden* **twinge** *in my leg as I was running.*

2 *My gran is in terrible* **pain** *after her fall last week.*

agony

painful adjective

Is your knee still **painful**?

sore
hurting
aching
tender

pale adjective

1 *She looked very tired and* **pale**.

white
white-faced
pallid
pasty

2 *He was wearing a* **pale** *blue shirt with dark blue jeans.*

light
faded
OPPOSITE **bright**

pant verb

He was **panting** *by the time he reached the top of the hill.*

to gasp
to gasp for breath
to puff
to huff and puff

part noun

1 *He kept one* **part** *of the cake for himself.*

a bit
a piece
a portion
a section

2 *We have completed the first* **part** *of our journey.*

a stage
a phase

3 *This is a beautiful* **part** *of the country.*

an area
a region

4 *Which* **part** *of the city do you live in?*

an area
a district

particular adjective

1 *There was one* **particular** *dress that she really liked.*

specific
special

a
b
c
d
e
f
g
h
i
j
k
l
m
n
o
p
q
r
s
t
u
v
w
x
y
z

A
B
C
D
E
F
G
H
I
J
K
L
M

N
O
P
Q
R
S
T
U
V
W
X
Y
Z

2 *She has her own **particular** way of writing.*
individual
personal
special
unique

partner noun
*Choose a **partner** to work with on the project.*
a friend
a companion
a colleague
a helper

party noun
*Are you having a **party**?*
a birthday party
a celebration
a gathering
a disco
a dance

pass verb
1 *I **pass** this shop every day on my way to school.*
to go past
to go by
2 *We **passed** an old van which was driving slowly along the road.*
to overtake
3 *Could you **pass** me the salt, please?*
to hand
to give

passage noun
1 *We walked down a narrow **passage** to the kitchen.*
a corridor
a passageway
a walkway
2 *They say there's a secret **passage** under the castle.*
a tunnel

pat verb
*He **patted** the dog on the head.*
to touch
to stroke
to tap

path noun
*We walked along the **path**.*
a footpath
a track
a bridleway a path for horses

patient adjective
*It won't take very long, so please be **patient**.*
calm
tolerant
OPPOSITE **impatient**

pause verb

He paused before opening the door.

to stop
to wait
to hesitate

pause noun

Let's have a pause for lunch.

a break
an interval
a rest

pay noun

You will get your pay at the end of the week.

wages
salary

pay verb pays, paying, paid

1 *He paid a lot of money for that bike.*

to give
to spend
to fork out *(informal) He forked out a lot of money on that bike.*

2 *If you let me have the video now, I'll pay you tomorrow.*

to repay
to reimburse

peace noun

1 *After the war ended there was peace between the two countries.*

friendliness
an agreement
a truce

2 *We enjoyed the peace of the quiet evening.*

quiet
silence
peacefulness
calmness
stillness

peaceful adjective

It seemed very peaceful sitting on the bench in the sunshine.

quiet
calm
tranquil
OPPOSITE **noisy**

peculiar adjective

This cheese has a peculiar taste.

strange
funny
odd
curious
bizarre
OPPOSITE **normal**

people noun

1 *The streets were full of people.*

folk
men and women

a
b
c
d
e
f
g
h
i
j
k
l
m
n
o
p
q
r
s
t
u
v
w
x
y
z

A
B
C
D
E
F
G
H
I
J
K
L
M
N
O
P
Q
R
S
T
U
V
W
X
Y
Z

2 *The president was elected by the* **people** *of his country.*
the public
the population
the citizens

perfect adjective
1 *The sun is shining and it's a* **perfect** *day for a picnic.*
ideal
excellent
2 *This is a* **perfect** *piece of work.*
excellent
flawless
faultless

perform verb
1 *The children were excited to see an opera* **performed** *for the first time.*
to put on
to present
2 *The singers love* **performing** *in public.*
to act
to dance
to sing
to be on stage

perhaps adverb
Perhaps *we'll see you at the opera tomorrow.*
maybe
possibly

person noun
1 *I saw a* **person** *walking towards me.*
a man
a woman
an adult
a grown-up
a child

a teenager
a boy
a girl
a baby
a toddler
2 *He's a very unpleasant* **person**.
an individual
a character
a human being

personality noun
She's got a lovely **personality** *and is very polite.*
a character
a nature
a temperament
a disposition

to **harass**
to **hassle**
Use **nag** when you keep reminding someone to do something: *My mum keeps **nagging** me to do my homework.*

phone verb
*I **phoned** my grandma to tell her all about our trip to the opera.*
to **call**
to **ring**
to **telephone**
to **give someone a ring** (informal) *I **gave** my grandma **a ring**.*

photograph noun
*I took a **photograph** of my sister.*
a **photo**
a **picture**
a **shot**
a **snapshot**
a **snap**

pick verb
1 *I didn't know which cake to **pick**.*
to **choose**
to **select**
to **decide on**
to **single out**
2 *We **picked** some blackberries for tea.*
to **gather**
to **collect**
to **harvest**
3 *She **picked** a flower from the bush.*
to **pluck**
to **cut**
4 *She **picked** the book up off the floor.*
to **lift up**

persuade verb
1 *She **persuaded** her mum to take her to the opera.*
to **encourage**
to **urge**
to **talk someone into** *She talked **her mum into** taking her to the opera.*
2 *The kitten was hiding under a chair, and I tried to **persuade** it to come out.*
to **coax** *I tried to **coax** it out.*
to **entice** *I tried to **entice** it out.*

pester verb
*My little brother kept **pestering** me to play tennis with him.*
to **annoy**
to **bother**

a
b
c
d
e
f
g
h
i
j
k
l
m
n
o
p
q
r
s
t
u
v
w
x
y
z

A
B
C
D
E
F
G
H
I
J
K
L
M
N
O
P
Q
R
S
T
U
V
W
X
Y
Z

picture noun

WORD WEB

Some types of **picture**:

a caricature
a funny picture
of a real person

a cartoon

a drawing

an illustration

an image
a picture in
a film or on
the computer

a painting

a photograph

a picture
in a book

a portrait
a picture
of a person

a sketch
a rough
drawing

a painting

a portrait

a photograph

a landscape

a caricature

a sketch

A
B
C
D
E
F
G
H
I
J
K
L
M
N
O
P
Q
R
S
T
U
V
W
X
Y
Z

piece noun

1 *She gave me a huge* **piece** *of cake.*

a **bit**

a **slice**

A **sliver** is a thin piece: *She cut herself a tiny* **sliver** *of cake.*

A **wedge** is a thick piece: *He was eating a huge* **wedge** *of chocolate cake.*

A **square** is a small, square piece: *Would you like a* **square** *of chocolate?*

A **lump, chunk, block,** or **slab** is a big, thick piece: *There was a big* **slab** *of concrete in the road.*

2 *We need another* **piece** *of wood.*

a **bit**

a **block**

a **plank**

3 *She handed me a* **piece** *of paper.*

a **bit**

a **sheet**

A **scrap** is a small piece of paper: *I wrote his phone number on a small* **scrap** *of paper.*

4 *We need a new* **piece** *of glass for that window.*

a **sheet**

a **pane**

5 *There were* **pieces** *of broken cup all over the kitchen floor.*

a **bit**

a **chip**

A **fragment** is a very small piece: *There were some tiny* **fragments** *of glass on the floor.*

6 *My dress was torn to* **pieces**.

shreds *My dress was torn to* **shreds**.

pile noun

There was a **pile** *of dirty clothes on the floor.*

a **heap**

a **mound**

a **mass**

a **stack**

pillar noun

The roof was held up by large stone **pillars**.

a **column**

a **post**

a **support**

pity noun

1 *She felt great* **pity** *for the hungry children.*

sympathy

understanding

2 *The soldiers showed no* **pity** *to their enemies.*

mercy

kindness

compassion

3 *It's a* **pity** *you can't come to the party.*

a **shame**

place noun

1 *A cross marks the* **place** *where the treasure is buried.*

a **spot**

a **position**

a **point**

a **location**

a **site**

2 *Our school is in a very nice* **place**.

an **area**

a **district**

a **neighbourhood**

a **town**

a **city**

a **village**

3 *Save me a* **place** *next to you.*

a **chair**

a **seat**

plain adjective

*The food in the hotel was quite **plain**.*

ordinary
simple
basic
not fancy
dull

plan noun

1 *He has a **plan** for the weekend.*

an idea
a scheme
a plot
a schedule

2 *We drew a **plan** of the town to show where we all live.*

a map
a diagram
a drawing
a chart
a sketch

3 *I made a **plan** for my story.*

a framework
a structure

plan verb

1 *When do you **plan** to leave?*

to intend
to aim

2 *He thinks they are **planning** to go to the park without him.*

to plot
to scheme

3 *We need to **plan** this trip very carefully.*

to organize
to arrange
to prepare for

plane noun see aircraft

plant noun

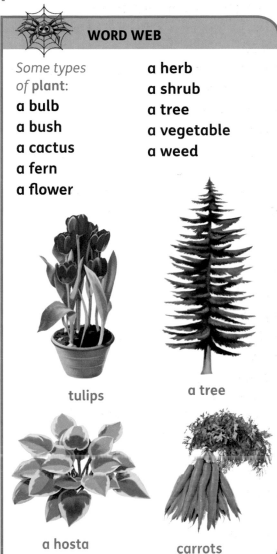

WORD WEB

Some types of **plant**:
a bulb
a bush
a cactus
a fern
a flower
a herb
a shrub
a tree
a vegetable
a weed

tulips

a tree

a hosta

carrots

play noun

*The children are putting on a **play** at the end of term.*

a show
a performance
a pantomime
a drama
a **comedy** a funny play
a **tragedy** a sad play

a
b
c
d
e
f
g
h
i
j
k
l
m
n
o
p
q
r
s
t
u
v
w
x
y
z

A
B
C
D
E
F
G
H
I
J
K
L
M
N
O
P
Q
R
S
T
U
V
W
X
Y
Z

play verb

1 *The children were* **playing** *on the beach.*

to have fun

to enjoy yourself *They were* **enjoying** *themselves.*

to amuse yourself *They were* **amusing** *themselves.*

2 *Manchester United* **play** *Liverpool next week.*

to take on

to compete against

to oppose

3 *She* **played** *a tune on the piano.*

to perform

to act

playful adjective

Kittens can be **playful** *and great fun.*

lively

mischievous

frisky

fun-loving

cheeky

OPPOSITE **serious**

pleasant adjective

1 *We had a very* **pleasant** *day on the beach.*

lovely

enjoyable

wonderful

fantastic

delightful

2 *He seems a very* **pleasant** *boy.*

friendly

kind

likeable

Use **thoughtful** for someone who thinks about other people: *It was very* **thoughtful** *of you to buy me a present.*

Use **charming** or **polite** for someone who behaves well and isn't rude to people: *Now remember you must be* **polite** *to all your relatives.*

3 *The weather was very* **pleasant** *and warm for the time of year.*

lovely

fine

beautiful

warm

sunny

glorious

wonderful

OPPOSITE **unpleasant**

pleased adjective

I was **pleased** *that so many people came to my party.*

happy

glad

joyful

Use **delighted** or **thrilled** when you are very pleased about something: *I was* **thrilled** *when I won the first prize!*

Use **grateful** or **thankful** when you are pleased because someone has been kind to you: *I'm very* **grateful** *for all your help.*

OPPOSITE **annoyed**

pleasure noun

She smiled with **pleasure** *when she won first prize in the spelling bee.*

happiness

enjoyment

contentment

amusement

Use **delight** or **joy** for a feeling of great pleasure: *His face lit up with* **delight** *when he saw his family waiting for him.*

plot verb

*I knew they were **plotting** to steal the jewels from the palace.*

to plan

to scheme

plot noun

*They had a secret **plot** to steal the money.*

a plan

a scheme

a conspiracy

plump adjective

*The shopkeeper was a small, **plump** man.*

fat

Use **tubby**, **chubby**, or **podgy** for someone who is slightly fat in a nice way: *There was a **chubby**, smiling baby in the buggy.*

Use **stout** or **portly** for an older person who is quite fat: *Uncle Toby was a **portly** man with a round, smiling face.*

Use **overweight** or **obese** for someone who is so fat that they are unhealthy: *It's important to exercise so you don't become **overweight**.*

OPPOSITE thin

poem noun

WORD WEB

*Some types of **poem**:*

an acrostic

a calligram

a cinquain

a haiku

a limerick

a nursery rhyme

a rap

a sonnet

point noun

1 *Be careful, those scissors have a very sharp **point**.*

an end

a tip

2 *We soon reached the **point** where the two roads met.*

a place

a spot

a situation

a location

3 *At that **point** I did not know about the treasure.*

a time

a moment

a stage

4 *What is the **point** of this game?*

the purpose

the aim

the object

the use

point verb

1 *He **pointed** towards the castle.*

to indicate

to gesture towards

2 *I **pointed** the hose at the paddling pool.*

to aim

to direct

poisonous adjective

1 *Some toadstools are **poisonous** so please don't eat them.*

harmful

toxic

Use **deadly** or **lethal** when something is so poisonous that it can kill you: *Arsenic is a **deadly** poison.*

2 *She was bitten by a **poisonous** snake.*

venomous

a
b
c
d
e
f
g
h
i
j
k
l
m
n
o
p
q
r
s
t
u
v
w
x
y
z

A
B
C
D
E
F
G
H
I
J
K
L
M
N
O
P
Q
R
S
T
U
V
W
X
Y
Z

poke verb

1 *He poked the seaweed with a stick.*

to prod
to push
to jab

2 *She poked me in the back.*

to nudge
to dig
to prod
to elbow

polite adjective

He's very polite and always says thank you.

well-mannered
well-behaved
respectful
courteous
civil
OPPOSITE **rude**

poor adjective

1 *His mother and father were very poor when they were young.*

Hard up is an informal way of saying that someone doesn't have much money to spend: *My dad's a bit hard up at the moment, so there's no point asking him for a new bike.*

Use **penniless** or **broke** for someone who does not have any money to spend: *I can't go to the fair because I'm absolutely broke!*

Use **needy** or **poverty-stricken** for someone who is very poor and doesn't have enough money for food: *We collect money to help poverty-stricken families in poor countries.*
OPPOSITE **rich**

2 *This is very poor work.*

bad
careless
sloppy
OPPOSITE **good**

popular adjective

He is a popular TV presenter and we watch him every week.

famous
well-known
well-liked
OPPOSITE **unpopular**

portion noun

1 *She gave me a huge portion of chips.*

a helping
a serving

2 *I only got a small portion of pie.*

a piece
a slice

positive adjective

I am positive I saw him at the supermarket.

certain
sure
convinced

possessions noun

We lost all our possessions in the fire.

belongings
property
things

possible adjective

It is possible that it will rain later.

likely
conceivable
feasible
OPPOSITE **impossible**

post noun

1 *The fence is supported by wooden posts.*

a pole
a stake

2 *Did you get any **post** this morning?*

mail
letters
parcels

poster noun

*We put up a **poster** to tell people about our concert.*

a notice
a sign
an announcement
an advertisement

postpone verb

*We **postponed** the match because of rain.*

to put off
to cancel
to delay

pour verb

1 *I **poured** some orange juice into a glass.*

to tip

2 *Water **poured** over the edge of the bath.*

to run
to spill

Use **splash** when water is pouring noisily: *Water from the roof was **splashing** down into the puddles below.*

Use **stream** or **gush** when a lot of water is pouring: *A huge jet of water **gushed** out of the burst pipe.*

3 *It was **pouring** with rain.*

to teem
to pelt down
to bucket down

power noun

1 *The police have the **power** to arrest thieves.*

the right
the authority

2 *In stories, magicians have special **powers**.*

an ability
a skill
a talent

3 *The **power** of the wave destroyed the building.*

force
strength
might
energy

powerful adjective

1 *He was a rich and **powerful** king.*

mighty
all-powerful

2 *The lion had **powerful** jaws.*

strong
mighty
great
OPPOSITE **weak**

practise verb

1 *I need to **practise** my speech.*

to go through
to run through
to work on
to rehearse

2 *The team meets once a week to **practise**.*

to train

praise verb

*Our teacher **praised** us for working so hard.*

to congratulate
to commend
to compliment
OPPOSITE **criticize**

a b c d e f g h i j k l m n o **p** q r s t u v w x y z

A
B
C
D
E
F
G
H
I
J
K
L
M
N
O
P
Q
R
S
T
U
V
W
X
Y
Z

precious adjective

1 *The necklace that my granny gave me is very **precious**.*

valuable

expensive

priceless

2 *I have a special box for all my **precious** possessions.*

prized

treasured

cherished

much-loved

precise adjective

*Please measure out the **precise** amount.*

exact

correct

right

accurate

prepare verb

1 *We are all busy **preparing** for the party.*

to get ready

to make preparations

to make arrangements

to plan

2 *I helped my mum **prepare** lunch.*

to make

to cook

present noun

*I got some lovely **presents** for my birthday.*

a gift

present verb

1 *She **presented** the prize to the winner.*

to give

to hand

to award

2 *Who will **present** the show tonight?*

to introduce

to host

press verb

*Don't **press** any of the buttons.*

to push

to touch

pretend verb

1 *Alice was in disguise, **pretending** to be a spy!*

to put it on

to fake

to play-act

2 *Let's **pretend** we're pirates.*

to imagine

to make believe

to play

pretty adjective

1 *You look **pretty** today.*

lovely

beautiful

attractive

Use **stunning** or **gorgeous** for someone who is very pretty: *My sister looked **stunning** in her wedding dress.*

2 *What a **pretty** little cottage!*

quaint

charming

delightful

OPPOSITE **ugly**

prick verb

*I **pricked** my finger on a needle.*

to jab

to stab

to pierce

prison noun

*The thief was sent to **prison** for ten years.*

jail
a cell
a dungeon

prisoner noun

*The **prisoners** were given bread and water.*

a convict
an inmate
a captive
a hostage a person taken prisoner by a kidnapper

private adjective

*1 They have their own **private** beach.*
personal
*2 You mustn't read her **private** letters.*
confidential
personal
secret
*3 We found a nice **private** spot for a picnic.*
hidden
secluded
quiet
isolated

prize noun

*I hope I win a **prize** at the school raffle.*

an award
a trophy
a cup
a medal

problem noun

*1 The lack of food was going to be a **problem**.*
a difficulty
a worry
trouble

*2 We had some difficult maths **problems** to solve.*
a question
*3 We solved the **problem** of the missing shoe.*
a mystery
a riddle
a puzzle
an enigma

prod verb

*1 She **prodded** the hole with a stick.*
to poke
to push
to jab
*2 Someone **prodded** me in the back.*
to nudge
to dig
to poke
to elbow

produce verb

*1 This factory **produces** furniture for offices.*
to make
to manufacture
to assemble
*2 Farmers **produce** food for us.*
to grow
*3 She **produced** a photo from her bag.*
to bring out
to take out

promise verb

*Do you **promise** that you will be home by five o'clock?*
to give your word
to swear
to vow
to guarantee

a b c d e f g h i j k l m n o **p** q r s t u v w x y z

143

A
B
C
D
E
F
G
H
I
J
K
L
M
N
O
P
Q
R
S
T
U
V
W
X
Y
Z

proper adjective

1 *Please put the book back in its* **proper** *place.*
correct
right
precise
2 *Can we have a ride in a* **proper** *boat?*
real
genuine

protect verb

1 *The bird always* **protects** *its chicks.*
to defend
to guard
to look after
to shield
2 *The hedge* **protected** *us from the wind.*
to shelter
to shield

protest verb

The children **protested** *when the teacher said they had to stay indoors.*
to complain
to object

proud adjective

Her parents felt very **proud** *when she went up to collect her prize.*
pleased
happy
delighted
honoured
OPPOSITE **ashamed**

prove verb

Can you **prove** *that you live here?*
to show
to establish
to demonstrate

prowl verb

The tiger **prowled** *round the tree.*
to creep
to slink

public adjective

This is a **public** *beach, not a private one, and everyone can use it.*
open
communal
shared
OPPOSITE **private**

publish verb

The school **publishes** *a magazine for us to read once a term.*
to bring out
to produce
to issue
to print

pull verb

1 *We* **pulled** *the heavy box across the floor.*
to drag
to haul
to lug
2 *I got hold of the handle and* **pulled** *hard.*
to tug
to yank
to heave
3 *The magician* **pulled** *a bunch of flowers out of a hat.*
to take
to lift
to draw
to produce

4 *I managed to* **pull** *the book out of her hands.*

to tear

to wrench

to drag

to rip

5 *The car was* **pulling** *a caravan.*

to tow

to draw

punch verb

That boy **punched** *me!*

to hit

to thump

to wallop

to strike

punish verb

The teachers will **punish** *you if you misbehave.*

to discipline

to make an example of

pupil noun

This school has about 500 **pupils**.

a schoolchild

a schoolboy

a schoolgirl

a student

pure adjective

1 *He was wearing a crown made of* **pure** *gold.*

real

solid

2 *We bought a carton of* **pure** *orange juice.*

natural

3 *The water here is lovely and* **pure**.

clean

clear

fresh

unpolluted

purse noun

Always keep your money in a **purse**.

a wallet

a bag

push verb

1 *The door will open if you* **push** *harder.*

to press

to shove

to apply pressure

2 *I* **pushed** *all the clothes into the bag.*

to force

to stuff

to stick

to ram

to squeeze

to jam

to cram

3 *We* **pushed** *the table into the corner.*

to move

to shove

to drag

4 *We* **pushed** *the trolley towards the checkout.*

to wheel

to trundle

to roll

5 *Someone* **pushed** *me in the back.*

to shove

to nudge

to prod

to poke

to elbow

a b c d e f g h i j k l m n o p q r s t u v w x y z

145

A
B
C
D
E
F
G
H
I
J
K
L
M
N
O
P
Q
R
S
T
U
V
W
X
Y
Z

6 *The boy* **pushed** *past me.*

to shove
to barge
to squeeze
to elbow your way

put verb puts, putting, put

OVERUSED WORD

Here are some more interesting words for **put**:

1 **Put** *all the pencils on my desk.*

to place
to leave

Use **position** when you put something carefully in a particular place:
He **positioned** *the clock so that he could see it from his bed.*

Use **arrange** when you put something in a place carefully so that it looks nice:
He **arranged** *the flowers in the vase.*

Use **pop** when you put something in a place quickly: *Why don't you quickly* **pop** *your bike in the shed?*

Use **pile** or **stack** when you put things in a pile: *I* **stacked** *the papers on my desk.*

Use **drop, dump, deposit,** or **plonk** when you put something in a place carelessly:
She ran in and **dumped** *her school bag on the floor.*

2 *I* **put** *a coin into the slot.*

to slide
to insert

3 *He* **put** *all the dirty clothes back into his bag.*

to shove
to push
to stick
to bung
to stuff

puzzle noun

1 *I like doing the* **puzzles** *in my comic.*

a brainteaser
a problem

2 *The disappearance of the keys was still a* **puzzle***.*

a mystery

4 *He* **put** *some sugar on his cereal.*

to sprinkle
to scatter

5 *Can you* **put** *some water on these plants?*

to spray
to sprinkle
to pour

6 *I* **put** *some butter on my bread.*

to spread

7 *We* **put** *all the pictures on the table so that we could see them.*

to lay
to lay out
to set out
to spread out
to arrange

8 *She* **put** *her bike against the wall.*

to lean
to rest
to stand
to prop

9 *They have* **put** *some new lights on the outside of the school*

to fix
to attach
to install
to fit

10 *You can* **put** *your car in the car park.*

to park
to leave

Qq

quake verb

*The rabbits were **quaking** in the cold so we took them into the house.*

to shake
to tremble
to quiver
to shiver
to shudder

quality noun

*The children have produced some work of very high **quality**.*

a standard
a class

quarrel verb

*What are you two **quarrelling** about?*

to argue
to disagree
to squabble

Use **fight** when people argue in a very angry or serious way: *The two brothers **fought** all the time and didn't get on at all.*

Use **fall out** when people quarrel and stop being friends: *I've **fallen out** with my best friend.*

Use **bicker** when people quarrel about little things: *The two girls were **bickering** over how many stickers they had.*

quarrel noun

*She had a **quarrel** with her brother.*

an argument
a disagreement
a squabble

A **row** is a loud quarrel: *I had a big **row** with my parents.*

A **fight** is an angry, serious quarrel: *We had a really big **fight** about who should have the main part in the play.*

question noun

*No one could answer my **question**.*

a query
an enquiry

queue noun

1 *There was a long **queue** of people waiting for tickets.*

a line

2 *There was a long **queue** of cars on the road.*

a line
a tailback

A
B
C
D
E
F
G
H
I
J
K
L
M
N
O
P
Q
R
S
T
U
V
W
X
Y
Z

quick adjective

1 *It was quite a quick journey and we arrived early.*

fast
speedy
swift
rapid

2 *He made a quick recovery from his illness.*

rapid
speedy

Use **instant** or **immediate** for something that happens very quickly: *The programme was an instant success.*

3 *He was walking at a quick pace as he was late for school.*

brisk
fast
swift

4 *We had a quick lunch and then left.*

hasty
hurried
brief

5 *They only came for a quick visit.*

short
brief
fleeting

quiet adjective

1 *Our teacher told us to be quiet.*

silent
hushed
OPPOSITE **noisy**

2 *We found a quiet place for our picnic.*

peaceful
calm
isolated
tranquil
OPPOSITE **crowded**

3 *She's a very quiet girl.*

reserved
placid
shy
timid
OPPOSITE **noisy**

4 *I listened to some quiet music.*

low
soft
OPPOSITE **loud**

quite adverb

1 *The water's quite warm so we can go swimming.*

fairly
pretty
reasonably
rather

2 *I'm not quite sure that I will be able to come to the party.*

completely
totally
absolutely
fully

Rr

rain noun

*There could be some **rain** later.*

a shower

Drizzle is very light rain: *The rain had slowed down to just a light **drizzle**.*

A **downpour** is a heavy shower of rain: *We got soaked when we got caught in a **downpour**.*

A **storm** is heavy rain with thunder: *That night there was a terrible **storm**.*

WRITING TIPS

Here are some useful words for writing about the **rain**:

- A **fine**, **light** rain was falling outside.
- There was **steady** rain all day.
- There were strong winds and **heavy** rain during the night.
- **Torrential** rain can cause flooding.
- The rain **poured down** all day.
- I heard rain **pattering** on the roof.

rain verb

*It's still **raining**.*

Use **drizzle** or **spit** when it is not raining very hard: *It was only **spitting** so we decided to carry on with our walk.*

Use **pour** when it is raining a lot: *We can't go outside! It's **pouring**!*

ran verb past tense *see* run

rang verb past tense *see* ring

reach verb

1 *I **reached** out my hand to pick up the basket.*
to stretch

2 *Can you **reach** the book?*
to touch
to grasp
to get hold of

3 *It was dark when we **reached** London.*
to arrive at/in
*It was dark when we **arrived** in London.*

read verb reads, reading, read

*I **read** a magazine while I was waiting.*

Use **look at**, **flick through**, and **browse through** when you read something quickly: *I **flicked through** the address book until I found her address.*

Use **read through** when you read all of something: *Make sure you **read through** the instructions.*

Use **study** or **pore over** when you read something very carefully: *Ben spent hours **poring over** the map.*

ready adjective

1 *Are you **ready** to leave?*
prepared
all set
waiting

a
b
c
d
e
f
g
h
i
j
k
l
m
n
o
p
q
r
s
t
u
v
w
x
y
z

149

A
B
C
D
E
F
G
H
I
J
K
L
M
N
O
P
Q
R
S
T
U
V
W
X
Y
Z

2 *Your goods are* **ready** *for you now.*

available

3 *Is lunch* **ready***?*

prepared
cooked

real adjective

1 *Is that a* **real** *diamond?*

genuine
authentic
OPPOSITE **artificial**

2 *Is Tiny your* **real** *name?*

actual
proper
OPPOSITE **false**

3 *She had never felt* **real** *sadness before.*

true
sincere

realistic adjective

We used fake blood, but it looked quite *realistic.*

lifelike
natural
authentic
OPPOSITE **unrealistic**

realize verb

I suddenly **realized** *that I had lost my phone.*

to know
to understand
to become aware
to notice
to see

really adverb

1 *The water's* **really** *cold!*

very
extremely

2 *Tom apologized, but I don't think he's* **really** *sorry.*

truly
honestly
genuinely

3 *Is your dad* **really** *a spy?*

actually

reason noun

1 *There must be a* **reason** *why this plant has died.*

a cause
an explanation

2 *What was your* **reason** *for telling us these lies?*

a motive

reasonable adjective

1 *It is* **reasonable** *to expect you to help with the work.*

fair
right
OPPOSITE **unreasonable**

2 *Let's try and discuss this in a* **reasonable** *way.*

sensible
rational
mature
OPPOSITE **irrational**

3 *You can earn a* **reasonable** *amount of money.*

fair
quite good
respectable

rebel verb

The other team **rebelled** *against the referee's decision.*

to revolt
to rise up

to mutiny
to disobey orders

receive verb

1 *I* **received** *some lovely presents.*
to get
to be given *I* **was given** *some lovely presents.*
2 *How much money do you* **receive** *each week for doing the paper round?*
to get
to earn
OPPOSITE **give**

recent adjective

Her **recent** *film is not as good as the others.*
new
latest
current
up-to-date

reckon verb

I **reckon** *our side will win.*
to think
to believe
to feel sure

recognize verb

Would you **recognize** *that man if you saw him again?*
to remember
to know
to identify

recommend verb

1 *A lot of people have* **recommended** *this book to me.*
to suggest
to speak highly of *A lot of people have* **spoken highly of** *this book.*

2 *I* **recommend** *that you should see a doctor.*
to suggest
to advise *I* **advise** *you to see a doctor.*

record noun

We kept a **record** *of the birds we saw on holiday.*
an account
a diary
a list
a journal
a log

recover verb

Have you **recovered** *from your illness?*
to get better
to get well
to recuperate
to get over

red adjective

1 *She was wearing a* **red** *dress.*
crimson
scarlet
maroon
2 *Her cheeks were* **red** *when she came in from the cold.*
rosy
glowing
flushed

reduce verb

1 *She* **reduced** *her speed when she saw the police car.*
to decrease
2 *We want to* **reduce** *the amount of litter in the playground.*
to lessen
to cut down

a
b
c
d
e
f
g
h
i
j
k
l
m
n
o
p
q
r
s
t
u
v
w
x
y
z

A
B
C
D
E
F
G
H
I
J
K
L
M
N
O
P
Q
R
S
T
U
V
W
X
Y
Z

3 *The school shop has **reduced** some of its prices.*
to lower
to cut
Use **slash** when a price is reduced a lot: *That shop is closing down, so all the prices have been **slashed**.*
Use **halve** when something is reduced by half: *The price was **halved** from £10 to £5.*
OPPOSITE **increase**

refreshed adjective
*I felt **refreshed** after my rest.*
invigorated
restored
revived
enlivened

refreshing adjective
1 *I had a lovely **refreshing** shower.*
invigorating
energizing
2 *I need a **refreshing** drink.*
cooling
thirst-quenching

refuse verb
*I offered to take him to the party, but he **refused**.*
to say no *He **said no**.*
to decline *He **declined**.*
to be unwilling *He **was unwilling**.*
OPPOSITE **accept**

region noun
*These animals only live in hot **regions**.*
an area
a place
a zone

regular adjective
1 *You should take **regular** exercise.*
frequent
daily
weekly
2 *The postman was on his **regular** delivery round.*
normal
usual
customary
3 *The drummer kept a **regular** rhythm.*
even
steady
OPPOSITE **irregular**

rehearse verb
1 *We **rehearsed** for the concert all afternoon.*
to practise
to prepare
2 *I think you should **rehearse** your speech.*
to go through
to run through

relax verb
1 *I like to **relax** after school.*
to rest
to unwind
to take it easy
2 ***Relax**, there's nothing to worry about.*
to calm down
to not panic *Don't panic!*

release verb
*They **released** the animals from the cage.*
to free
to liberate
to set free *They **set** the animals **free**.*
to turn loose *They **turned** the animals **loose**.*

reliable adjective

*I'm surprised that Joshua is late, he's usually so **reliable**.*

dependable
responsible
trustworthy
OPPOSITE **unreliable**

relieved adjective

*I was very **relieved** when I heard that no one was hurt after the accident.*

happy
glad
thankful

religion noun

*Different people around the world follow different **religions**.*

a belief
a faith
a creed

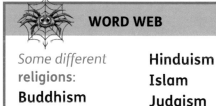

WORD WEB

Some different religions:
Buddhism
Christianity
Hinduism
Islam
Judaism
Sikhism

reluctant adjective

*I was **reluctant** to walk home because it was raining.*

unwilling
unhappy
not keen
hesitant
slow
OPPOSITE **keen**

rely on verb

1 *The young chicks **rely on** their mother for food.*

to depend on
to need

2 *We know we can always **rely on** you to help us.*

to trust
to count on

remains noun

1 *We visited the **remains** of a Roman fort.*

ruins
remnants

2 *We gave the **remains** of the food to the dog.*

the leftovers
the rest

remark verb

*I **remarked** that it was a nice day.*

to comment
to mention
to observe
to point out

remarkable adjective

*This was a **remarkable** achievement.*

extraordinary
amazing
astonishing
incredible
OPPOSITE **ordinary**

remember verb

1 *I can't **remember** his name.*

to recall
to recollect

a
b
c
d
e
f
g
h
i
j
k
l
m
n
o
p
q
r
s
t
u
v
w
x
y
z

2 *I'm going to give you my phone number, and you must **remember** it.*

to learn

to memorize

to make a mental note of

OPPOSITE **forget**

remind verb

*Seeing her with her swimming kit **reminded** me that I needed mine.*

to jog someone's memory *Seeing her with her swimming kit **jogged my memory**.*

remove verb

1 *Please **remove** this rubbish from your desk.*

to move

to take away

to get rid of

2 *He opened the drawer and **removed** some of the papers.*

to take out

to lift out

to extract

3 *She carefully **removed** the stamp from the envelope.*

to take off

to tear off

to cut off

to detach

4 *Someone had **removed** the door handle.*

to take off

to break off

to snap off

5 *He walked into the house and **removed** his shoes.*

to take off

to kick off

to slip off

to pull off

6 *We scrubbed the walls to **remove** the dirt.*

to wipe off

to scrape off

to scratch off

to rub off

7 *I **removed** her name from the list.*

to cross out

to rub out

to erase

to delete

8 *I **removed** some files from my computer.*

to delete

to wipe

9 *The police **removed** him from the building.*

to evict

to throw out

repeat verb

*Could you **repeat** that, please?*

to say again *Could you **say** that **again**, please?*

reiterate *Mum **reiterated** that we must be home by seven o'clock.*

reply noun

*I called her name, but there was no **reply**.*

an answer

a response

reply verb

*I asked him another question, but he didn't **reply**.*

to answer

to respond

report noun

1 *We had to write a **report** of what had happened.*

an account

a description

2 There was a **report** about our school in the local newspaper.

an article

a story

rescue verb

1 They **rescued** the prisoners from the dungeon.

to free

to release

to liberate

to set free He set the prisoners free.

2 A lifeboat was sent out to **rescue** the men on the sinking boat.

to save

respect verb

I **respect** my grandparents as they are older than me.

to look up to

to admire

to think highly of

respect noun

You should always treat other people with respect.

consideration

thoughtfulness

courtesy

politeness

responsible adjective

1 You are **responsible** for feeding the fish.

in charge of You are in charge of feeding the fish.

2 Who is **responsible** for breaking this window?

to blame for Who is to blame for breaking this window?

guilty of Who is guilty of breaking this window?

3 We need a **responsible** person to look after the money.

sensible

reliable

trustworthy

OPPOSITE irresponsible

rest noun

1 I need a **rest**!

a break

a pause

a sit-down

a lie-down

A **breather** is a short rest to get your breath back: We stopped for a **breather** before continuing up the mountain.

2 The doctor says that I need plenty of **rest**.

sleep

relaxation

3 If you have finished, leave the **rest**.

the remainder

the leftovers

rest verb

We'll **rest** for half an hour before we continue.

to relax

to take it easy

to sit down

to lie down

to sleep

to have a nap

result noun

1 As a **result** of our good behaviour we got extra playtime.

a consequence

an outcome

2 I didn't see the match, but I know the **result**.

a score

a b c d e f g h i j k l m n o p q r s t u v w x y z

A
B
C
D
E
F
G
H
I
J
K
L
M
N
O
P
Q
R
S
T
U
V
W
X
Y
Z

retreat verb

*The soldiers **retreated** rapidly towards the fort.*

to go back
to move back
to withdraw
to flee

return verb

1 *We decided to **return** to the cave.*

to go back

2 *He left, and we didn't know if he would ever **return**.*

to come back
to reappear

reveal verb

1 *He opened the door and **revealed** a secret room.*

to expose
to show

2 *She drew back the curtain and **revealed** a statue of a man.*

to uncover
to unveil
to unmask

3 *Don't ever **reveal** our secret!*

to tell
to disclose
to let out *Don't ever **let** this secret **out**.*
to make known *Don't ever **make** this secret **known**.*

review noun

*I wrote a **review** of the book.*

an assessment
an evaluation
a judgement

revolting adjective

1 *The food was **revolting**.*

horrible
disgusting
tasteless
inedible

2 *What a **revolting** hat!*

horrible
vile
hideous
repulsive
OPPOSITE **pleasant**

rich adjective

*She dreamed of being **rich** and famous.*

wealthy
well-off
prosperous
OPPOSITE **poor**

ridiculous adjective

*That's a **ridiculous** thing to say!*

silly
absurd
foolish
stupid
ludicrous
preposterous
crazy
OPPOSITE **sensible**

right adjective

1 *All my answers were **right**.*

correct
accurate

Use **spot on** when something is exactly right: *I guessed he weighed 24 kilos, and I was **spot on**.*

2 *Is that the **right** time?*

exact

precise

3 *I haven't got the **right** books.*

appropriate

suitable

proper

4 *It's **right** to own up when you've been naughty.*

honest

fair

good

sensible

honourable

OPPOSITE **wrong**

ring noun

*We all stood in a **ring** with Emily in the middle.*

a circle

ring verb rings, ringing, rang

1 *I could hear bells **ringing**.*

to sound

Use **chime** or **peal** to describe the sound of large bells: *The church bells **chimed**.*

Use **tinkle** or **jingle** to describe the sound of small bells: *The bells around the horse's neck **jingled** as it trotted along.*

2 *I'll **ring** you later.*

to call

to phone

to telephone

rise verb rises, rising, rose

1 *I watched the balloon **rise** into the sky.*

to climb

to ascend

Use **soar** when something rises very high: *The eagle **soared** high into the sky.*

OPPOSITE **descend**

2 *The sun was **rising** when we got up.*

to come up

OPPOSITE **set**

3 *Bus fares are going to **rise** next week.*

to increase

to go up

OPPOSITE **fall**

river noun

*We walked along next to the **river**.*

A **stream** or **brook** is a small river: *There was a little **stream** at the bottom of the garden.*

A **canal** is a man-made river: *In the past, goods were transported along **canals**.*

WRITING TIPS

Here are some useful words for writing about **rivers**:

• *They sailed along the **wide**, **meandering** river.*

• *The river here is **broad** and **slow-moving**.*

• *They came to the edge of a **deep**, **fast-moving** river.*

• *The **mighty** river **flows** towards the sea.*

• *A river **winds** through the field.*

• *A **shallow** river **runs** through the middle of the forest.*

• *We watched the river **rushing** past.*

a
b
c
d
e
f
g
h
i
j
k
l
m
n
o
p
q
r
s
t
u
v
w
x
y
z

157

A
B
C
D
E
F
G
H
I
J
K
L
M
N
O
P
Q
R
S
T
U
V
W
X
Y
Z

road noun

1 *This is the **road** where I live.*

a street

an avenue

a close

2 *There is a narrow **road** between the two farms.*

a track

a path

a lane

an alley

3 *We drove along the **road** between Birmingham and London.*

a main road

a motorway

roar verb

*The crowd **roared** when he scored the goal.*

to bellow

to shout

to cry

to yell

robber noun

*The **robbers** escaped from the building.*

a burglar

a thief

a crook

a pickpocket

a shoplifter

rock noun

*He picked up a **rock** and hurled it into the sea.*

a stone

A **boulder** is a very big rock: *We had to climb over some huge **boulders**.*

rock verb

1 *The little boat **rocked** gently in the breeze.*

to sway

to swing

2 *The ship **rocked** violently in the storm.*

to roll

to toss

to pitch

roll verb

*The logs **rolled** down the hill.*

to spin

to tumble

room noun

*Is there enough **room** for me to sit down?*

space

rose verb past tense *see* rise

rotten adjective

1 *The wood was old and **rotten**.*

decayed

decomposed

OPPOSITE **sound**

2 *The meat was **rotten**.*

bad

Use **mouldy** for cheese: *There was some **mouldy** old cheese in the fridge.*

Use **off** for meat and fish: *We can't eat this meat. It's gone **off**.*

OPPOSITE **fresh**

3 *That was a **rotten** thing to do!*

nasty

unkind

mean

horrible

OPPOSITE **good**

rough adjective

1 *We jolted along the **rough** road.*

bumpy

uneven
stony
rocky
OPPOSITE **even**
2 *Sandpaper feels rough.*
coarse
scratchy
OPPOSITE **smooth**
3 *He spoke in a rough voice.*
gruff
husky
hoarse
OPPOSITE **soft**
4 *The sea was very rough.*
stormy
choppy
OPPOSITE **calm**
5 *Don't be so rough with your little brother.*
aggressive
boisterous
rowdy
violent
OPPOSITE **gentle**
6 *At a rough guess, there were 50 of us.*
approximate
estimated
OPPOSITE **exact**

row noun (rhymes with *cow*)
1 *I had a row with my sister.*
an argument
a quarrel
a squabble
a disagreement
a fight
2 *What's that terrible row?*
noise
din
racket
rumpus

row noun (rhymes with *toe*)
We stood in a straight row.
a line
a queue

rub verb
1 *He rubbed the paint to make it come off.*
to scratch
to scrape
2 *He rubbed the old coin to make it shine.*
to clean
to polish
rub out
She rubbed out what she had just written.
to erase
to remove
to delete

rubbish noun
1 *The rubbish is collected once a week.*
refuse
waste
garbage *(American)*
trash *(American)*
2 *There was rubbish all over the playground.*
litter
3 *The garage is full of old rubbish.*
junk
4 *You're talking rubbish!*
nonsense

rude adjective
1 *Don't be rude to your teacher.*
cheeky
impertinent
impudent
insolent
disrespectful

a b c d e f g h i j k l m n o p q r s t u v w x y z

159

2 *It's* **rude** *to interrupt people.*

bad-mannered

impolite

3 *They got told off for telling* **rude** *jokes.*

indecent

dirty

vulgar

OPPOSITE **polite**

ruin verb

1 *The storm* **ruined** *the farmers' crops.*

to spoil

to damage

to destroy

to wreck

2 *The bad weather* **ruined** *our holiday.*

to spoil

to mess up

rule noun

It is a school **rule** *that all children must wear uniform.*

a regulation

a law

rule verb

In the old days, a king **ruled** *the country.*

to govern

to control

to run

ruler noun

Who is the **ruler** *of this country?*

a monarch

a king or **queen**

a sovereign

an emperor

an empress

a president

run verb runs, running, ran

OVERUSED WORD

Here are some more interesting words for **run**:

1 *We* **ran** *across the field.*

Use **jog** if you run quite slowly: *I sometimes go* **jogging** *with my dad.*

Use **sprint**, **race**, **tear**, **charge**, or **fly** if you run as fast as you can: *I* **raced** *home.*

Use **rush**, **dash**, or **hurry** if you are running because you are in a hurry: *I* **dashed** *back home to pick up my PE kit.*

Use **career** if you are running fast and out of control: *The two boys came* **careering** *into the kitchen.*

2 *The dog* **ran** *towards us.*

to bound

to scamper

3 *The horses* **ran** *across the field.*

to trot

to canter

to gallop

4 *The little mouse* **ran** *into its hole.*

to scurry

to scuttle

5 *She* **runs** *a drama club after school.*

to manage

run away

I chased them but they **ran away**.

to escape

to get away

rush verb

I **rushed** *to the bus stop.*

to dash

to hurry

to run

Ss

sad adjective

OVERUSED WORD

Here are some more interesting words for **sad**:

1 *The little boy looked very* **sad**.

unhappy
upset
miserable
fed up
dejected
despondent
depressed
gloomy
glum
down in the dumps

Use **disappointed** if someone is sad because something has gone wrong: *I was really* **disappointed** *when we lost in the final*.

Use **tearful** if someone is sad and almost crying: *Amy was very* **tearful** *when her kitten died*.

Use **heartbroken** when someone is extremely sad: *I was* **heartbroken** *when my best friend moved to another town*.

2 *This is very* **sad** *news*.

upsetting
tragic
depressing
distressing
disappointing
OPPOSITE **happy**

safe adjective

1 *Is that cat* **safe** *from the mouse?*

secure
out of danger
out of harm's way
sheltered
protected
OPPOSITE **in danger**

2 *The building was destroyed, but all the people were* **safe**.

safe and sound
unharmed
unhurt
in one piece
OPPOSITE **hurt**

3 *Castles were very* **safe** *places*.

secure
well-protected
well-defended
impregnable
OPPOSITE **dangerous**

4 *Is this ladder* **safe**?

firm
secure
strong enough
OPPOSITE **dangerous**

5 *Tigers are wild animals and are never completely* **safe**.

harmless
tame
OPPOSITE **dangerous**

said verb

past tense *see* **say**

a b c d e f g h i j k l m n o p q r **s** t u v w x y z

161

A
B
C
D
E
F
G
H
I
J
K
L
M
N
O
P
Q
R
S
T
U
V
W
X
Y
Z

sail verb

1 *We're **sailing** to France tomorrow.*

to set sail

to go by ship

2 *We watched the yachts **sailing** on the lake.*

to float

to glide

to drift

to bob

3 *The huge ship **sailed** out of the harbour.*

to steam

to chug

same adjective

*All the houses on the street look the **same** to me.*

identical

similar

alike

OPPOSITE **different**

sang verb past tense *see* **sing**

sank verb past tense *see* **sink**

satisfactory adjective

*Your work is **satisfactory**, but I think you could do better.*

all right

OK

acceptable

fair

adequate

OPPOSITE **unsatisfactory**

save verb

1 *A firefighter climbed into the burning building to **save** her.*

Use **rescue** when you save someone from danger: *A lifeboat was sent out to **rescue** the men on the boat.*

Use **free**, **release**, or **liberate** when you save someone who is a prisoner: *She opened the cage and **liberated** the birds.*

2 *She was **saving** the money until she had enough to buy a camera.*

to keep

to put aside *I'm going to **put** this money **aside**.*

saw verb past tense *see* **see**

say verb says, saying, said

 OVERUSED WORD

Here are some more interesting words for **say**:

'It's time to leave,' she **said**.

Use **add** when someone says something more: *I've got some money,'* he said. *'About £5,'* he **added**.

Use **ask** or **enquire** when someone asks a question: *'How old are you?'* the teacher **asked**.

Use **complain** or **moan** when someone is not happy about something: *'You didn't wait for me,'* she **moaned.**

Use **confess** or **admit** when someone admits they have done something wrong: *'I'm afraid I've spent all your money,'* George **confessed**.

Use **suggest** when someone makes a suggestion: *'Let's go and find something to eat,'* Sarah **suggested**.

Use **announce** or **declare** when someone says something important: *'We must leave tomorrow,'* he **announced**.

Use **answer**, **reply**, or **respond** when someone is giving an answer: *George thought about the question, then* **answered**, *'No.'*

Use **shout**, **cry**, **yell**, **scream**, or **shriek** when someone says something very loudly: *'You idiot!'* **yelled** Matt.

Use **mutter**, **mumble**, **murmur**, or **whisper** when someone says something very quietly: *'I'm sorry,'* she **muttered** quietly.

Use **snap**, **growl**, or **snarl** when someone says something angrily: *'Be quiet!'* **snapped** Katie.

Use **stutter**, **stammer**, or **splutter** when someone has difficulty saying the words: *'I d-d-don't know,'* she **stammered**.

Use **laugh** if someone is laughing while they speak: *'That's so funny!'* he **laughed**.

Use **sneer**, **scoff**, or **jeer** if someone is making fun of another person: *'You'll never win the race on that old bike,'* Tim **scoffed**.

Use **chorus** when people say something together: *'Yes, Miss Edwards,'* **chorused** the girls.

A
B
C
D
E
F
G
H
I
J
K
L
M
N
O
P
Q
R
S
T
U
V
W
X
Y
Z

scare verb

*Some of the scenes in the movie really **scared** me.*

to frighten
to give someone a fright
to make someone jump

Use **terrify** when something scares you a lot: *The thought of starting at the new school **terrified** me.*

Use **startle** or **make someone jump** when something suddenly scares you: *The phone rang suddenly, which **made me jump**.*

scared adjective

*Are you **scared** of mice?*

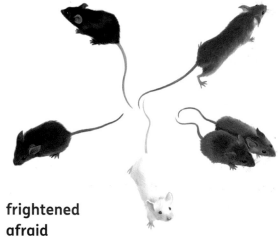

frightened
afraid

Use **terrified** or **petrified** when you are very scared: *I was absolutely **terrified** when I saw the giant.*

scary adjective

*The woods were **scary** at night and I didn't like to go in them.*

frightening

Use **eerie** or **spooky** when you think there might be ghosts: *It was really **eerie** being in the old castle at night.*

Use **terrifying** when something is very scary: *In front of us stood a **terrifying** monster.*

scrape verb

*We **scraped** the mud off our shoes.*

to rub
to clean
to scrub

scratch verb

1 *Mind you don't **scratch** the paint on the car.*

to damage
to scrape
to mark

2 *His head was itching so he **scratched** it.*

to rub

scream verb

1 *I **screamed** when I saw the spider.*

to cry out
to shriek
to squeal

2 *'Go away!' she **screamed**.*

to cry
to shout
to call
to yell
to shriek
to screech

sea noun

*They sailed across the **sea**.*

the ocean
the water
the waves
the deep

search verb

*I was **searching** for my watch as I'd lost it.*

to look for
to hunt for
to try to find

seat noun

*I sat down on a **seat** by the door.*

a chair

> ### WORD WEB
>
> *Some types of **seat**:*
>
> **an armchair**
> **a bench**
> **a high chair** a child's seat
> **a rocking chair**
> **a settee**
> **a sofa**
> **a stool**
>
> an armchair

secret adjective

1 *She wrote everything down in her **secret** diary.*

personal
private

2 *There is a **secret** garden behind the house.*

hidden
concealed
secluded

see verb sees, seeing, saw

1 *I **saw** a horse in the field.*

to notice

Use **observe** or **watch** when you look at something for quite a long time: *You can **observe** birds in your garden.*

Use **spot** or **spy** when you see something that is difficult to see: *We **spotted** a tiny ship on the horizon.*

Use **catch sight of**, **glimpse**, or **catch a glimpse of** when you see something very quickly and then it disappears: *I **caught a glimpse of** a deer as it ran through the forest.*

Use **witness** when you see a crime or accident: *Did anyone **witness** this accident?*

2 *I'm going to **see** my grandma tomorrow.*

to visit
to pay a visit to
to call on

3 *I **see** what you mean.*

to understand
to know

seem verb

*Everyone **seems** very happy today.*

to appear
to look
to sound

seize verb

1 *I **seized** the end of the rope.*

to grab
to take hold of
to clutch
to grasp

2 *The thief **seized** my bag and ran off.*

to grab
to snatch

a
b
c
d
e
f
g
h
i
j
k
l
m
n
o
p
q
r
s
t
u
v
w
x
y
z

A
B
C
D
E
F
G
H
I
J
K
L
M
N
O
P
Q
R
S
T
U
V
W
X
Y
Z

3 *The police* **seized** *the two men.*
to arrest
to catch
to capture

selfish adjective

You shouldn't be so **selfish.**
mean
self-centred
thoughtless
OPPOSITE **unselfish**

sense noun

That dog has got no **sense** *and does the silliest things.*
common sense
intelligence
brains

sensible adjective

1 *She is usually a very* **sensible** *girl.*
careful
thoughtful
level-headed
responsible
mature
wise
2 *That would be the* **sensible** *thing to do.*
logical
prudent
wise
OPPOSITE **stupid**

sensitive adjective

1 *Tom is feeling very* **sensitive** *about losing his phone as it was brand new.*
easily hurt
easily upset
touchy
OPPOSITE **insensitive**

2 *Don't use this cream if you have* **sensitive** *skin.*
delicate

separate adjective

1 *We need to keep the two piles* **separate.**
apart
2 *The two brothers sleep in* **separate** *bedrooms.*
different
OPPOSITE **together**

separate verb

1 **Separate** *the stickers into two piles.*
to divide
to split
to remove

2 *Alice and Samir wouldn't stop talking, so the teacher* **separated** *them.*
to move
to split up *The teacher* **split** *them* **up.**
to break up *The teacher* **broke** *them* **up.**

serious adjective

1 *The old man was looking very* **serious.**
sad
solemn
grave
thoughtful
OPPOSITE **cheerful**
2 *Are you* **serious** *about wanting to help?*
sincere
genuine
OPPOSITE **insincere**

3 *This is a very **serious** problem and we don't know how to fix it.*

important

significant

difficult

OPPOSITE **unimportant**

4 *Littering is **serious** problem in the city centre.*

bad

terrible

awful

dreadful

OPPOSITE **minor**

5 *She has a very **serious** illness and isn't able to work any more.*

bad

dangerous

life-threatening

OPPOSITE **minor**

set noun

*I need to get one more card, then I'll have the whole **set**.*

a collection

a series

set verb sets, setting, set

1 *The teacher forgot to **set** us any homework.*

to give

2 *We'll camp for the night when the sun **sets**.*

to go down

3 *Has the glue **set** yet?*

to harden

to solidify

shady adjective

*We found a **shady** place to eat our lunch.*

cool

shaded

OPPOSITE **sunny**

shake verb shakes, shaking, shook

1 *I picked up the money box and **shook** it.*

to rattle

2 *My granny **shook** her finger at me.*

to wave

to waggle

3 *The whole house seemed to **shake**.*

to move

to rock

to sway

to wobble

to vibrate

to shudder

4 *The old truck **shook** as it drove along the bumpy lane.*

to judder

to jolt

to rattle

5 *I was **shaking** with cold.*

to tremble

to quake

to quiver

to shiver

to shudder

a
b
c
d
e
f
g
h
i
j
k
l
m
n
o
p
q
r
s
t
u
v
w
x
y
z

167

shape noun

1 *In the darkness I could just see the* **shape** *of a building.*

the outline

2 *He's a powerful magician who can take on any* **shape** *he chooses.*

a form

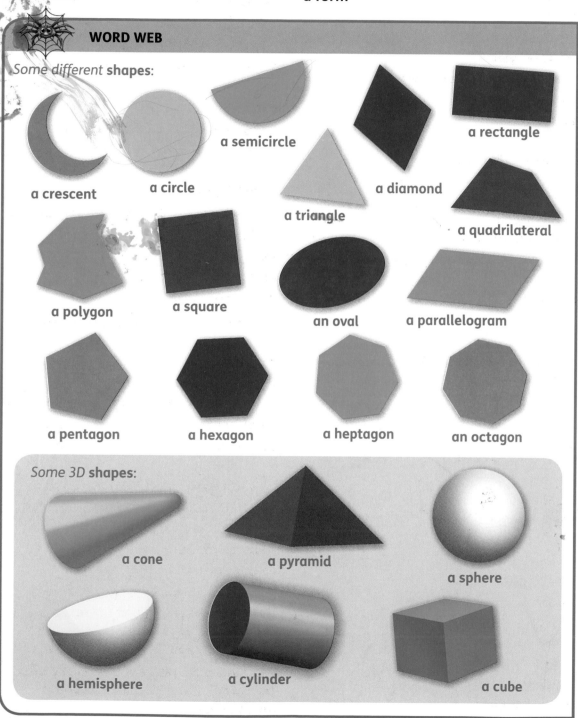

WORD WEB

Some different **shapes:**

a crescent

a circle

a semicircle

a diamond

a rectangle

a triangle

a quadrilateral

a polygon

a square

an oval

a parallelogram

a pentagon

a hexagon

a heptagon

an octagon

Some 3D **shapes:**

a cone

a pyramid

a sphere

a hemisphere

a cylinder

a cube

share noun

*Don't worry, you will get your **share** of the stickers.*

a part
a portion

share verb

*We **shared** the food between us.*

to divide
to split

sharp adjective

1 *Be careful, that knife is **sharp** and could hurt you.*

razor-sharp
OPPOSITE **blunt**

2 *It hurt our feet walking over the **sharp** rocks.*

pointed
jagged
OPPOSITE **smooth**

3 *A hedgehog's body is covered in **sharp** spines.*

prickly
spiky
OPPOSITE **smooth**

4 *There was a **sharp** bend in the road.*

sudden
tight
OPPOSITE **gradual**

5 *He's a very **sharp** boy.*

clever
intelligent
bright
brainy
quick
smart
brilliant
OPPOSITE **stupid**

shed noun

*There's a **shed** at the bottom of the garden.*

a hut
an outhouse
a shack

shed verb sheds, shedding, shed

1 *Some trees **shed** their leaves in the winter.*

to drop
to lose

2 *Snakes **shed** their old skin each year.*

to cast off

shelter noun

*The trees gave us some **shelter** from the rain.*

protection
refuge
cover

shelter verb

1 *We **sheltered** from the storm in an old barn.*

to hide
to stay safe

2 *The hedge **sheltered** us from the wind.*

to protect
to shield

shine verb shines, shining, shone

1 *The sun **shone** all day.*

to be out *The sun **was out** all day.*
to blaze down
to beat down

2 *I saw a light **shining** in the distance.*

Use **glow**, **glimmer**, **gleam**, or **shimmer** when something shines gently: *The light from the fire **glowed** softly in the darkness.*

Use **flash** when a light shines on and off: *The light from the lighthouse **flashed in** the darkness.*

A B C D E F G H I J K L M N O P Q R **S** T U V W X Y Z

Use **flicker**, **twinkle**, or **sparkle** when a light shines in an unsteady way, like a star: *The Christmas tree lights* **flickered** *and* **sparkled**.

Use **glint** or **glitter** when something made of metal or glass shines: *His sword* **glinted** *in the moonlight.*

shiny adjective

1 *We found a* **shiny** *new coin.*

bright
gleaming

2 *He was wearing* **shiny** *shoes.*

polished

3 *We printed our designs on* **shiny** *paper.*

glossy

OPPOSITE **dull**

shiver verb

1 *I was* **shivering** *with cold.*

to shake

2 *She was* **shivering** *with fear.*

to shake
to tremble
to quake
to quiver
to shudder

shock verb

1 *The explosion* **shocked** *everyone.*

to frighten
to alarm
to shake

2 *News of the accident* **shocked** *us all.*

to upset
to distress

3 *The swearing in the film* **shocked** *us.*

to offend
to disgust
to horrify

shocked adjective

1 *I felt quite* **shocked** *when I realized I had won.*

surprised
astonished
astounded
staggered

2 *The whole family was* **shocked** *when their pet rabbit died.*

upset
distressed
traumatized

3 *I was* **shocked** *when I heard the children swearing.*

disgusted
appalled
horrified

shoe noun

WORD WEB

Some types of **shoe**:

boots
plimsolls
pumps
sandals
slippers
trainers
wellingtons

pumps

slippers

trainers

plimsolls

shone verb past tense *see* **shine**

shook verb past tense *see* **shake**

shop noun
*You can buy comics in the **shop** on the corner.*
a store

WORD WEB

*Some big **shops**:*
a department store
a hypermarket
a supermarket

*Some other types of **shops**:*
a baker
a book shop
a boutique
a butcher
a chemist

a clothes shop
a delicatessen
a fishmonger
a florist
a gift shop
a grocer
an ironmonger
a jeweller
a music shop
a newsagent
a post office
a shoe shop
a toy shop

short adjective
1 *I'm quite **short** for my age.*
small
little
OPPOSITE **tall**
2 *It was a strange animal, with a long body and **short** legs.*
stumpy
stubby
OPPOSITE **long**
3 *It was just a **short** visit.*
brief
fleeting
quick

shout verb
*'You're here at last!' he **shouted**.*
to yell
to cry
to call
to bawl
to bellow
Use **scream** or **shriek** when someone is very frightened or excited: *'Help!' she **screamed**.*
Use **cheer** when people are happy about something: *'Hooray!' they **cheered**.*
Use **jeer** when people are making fun of someone: *'You're useless!' they **jeered**.*
OPPOSITE **whisper**

show noun
*We put on a school **show** at the end of term.*
a performance
a production
a play
a concert

show verb shows, showing, shown
1 *Shall I **show** you my new bike?*
to let someone see *I'll **let you see** my new bike.*
2 *He **showed** me the place where the accident happened.*
to point to
to indicate *He **indicated** the place where the accident happened.*
3 *We **showed** our work to the visitors.*
to display
to exhibit
4 *She **showed** me how to use the computer.*
to tell
to teach
to explain *She **explained** to me how to use the computer.*

a b c d e f g h i j k l m n o p q r **s** t u v w x y z

A
B
C
D
E
F
G
H
I
J
K
L
M
N
O
P
Q
R
S
T
U
V
W
X
Y
Z

shown verb past tense *see* **show**

shrivel verb

*The plants **shrivelled** in the heat.*

to dry up

to wither

shut verb shuts, shutting, shut

*She went out of the room and **shut** the door.*

to close

to fasten

to pull shut

to push shut

Use **lock** or **bolt** when you shut something and lock it: *He **bolted** the door securely.*

Use **slam** or **bang** when you shut something noisily: *She ran out and **slammed** the door.*

OPPOSITE **open**

shy adjective

*He was too **shy** to say that he knew the answer.*

nervous

timid

bashful

modest

sick adjective

1 *I stayed off school because I was **sick**.*

ill

unwell

poorly

2 *After eating all that chocolate I felt **sick**.*

queasy

side noun

1 *Some people were standing at one **side** of the field.*

an edge

2 *We waited at the **side** of the road.*

the edge

the verge

sign noun

1 *The **sign** for a dollar is $.*

a symbol

a logo

2 *There was a **sign** telling people to keep off the grass.*

a notice

a signpost

3 *I'll give you a **sign** when I'm ready for you to start.*

a signal

a gesture

silent adjective

1 *The hall was empty and **silent**.*

quiet

peaceful

noiseless

OPPOSITE **noisy**

2 *The teacher told us to be **silent**.*

quiet

OPPOSITE **talkative**

3 *I asked him some questions, but he remained **silent**.*

tight-lipped

silly adjective

1 *It's **silly** to go out in the rain.*

daft

foolish

stupid

unwise

2 *Please stop this **silly** behaviour.*

childish

immature

3 *Why are you wearing such* **silly** *clothes?*

ridiculous
peculiar
odd
unsuitable

similar adjective

The two girls look quite **similar**.

alike
identical
the same
OPPOSITE different

simple adjective

1 *That's a* **simple** *question.*

easy
straightforward
clear
obvious
OPPOSITE difficult

2 *We used quite a* **simple** *design for our poster.*

plain
not fancy
OPPOSITE elaborate

sing verb sings, singing, sang

1 *He was* **singing** *quietly to himself.*

to hum

2 *The birds were* **singing** *in the trees.*

to chirp
to cheep
to twitter
to warble

sink verb sinks, sinking, sank

The ship **sank** *in a storm.*

to go down
to founder
to be submerged *The ship was* **submerged**.

site noun

This would be a very good **site** *for the new school.*

a place
a spot
a position
a location

situation noun

1 *This is a terrible* **situation**.

a state of affairs

2 *I wouldn't like to be in your* **situation**.

a position

size noun

What is the **size** *of this room?*

the measurements
the dimensions
the length
the width
the breadth
the height

a
b
c
d
e
f
g
h
i
j
k
l
m
n
o
p
q
r
s
t
u
v
w
x
y
z

A
B
C
D
E
F
G
H
I
J
K
L
M
N
O
P
Q
R
S
T
U
V
W
X
Y
Z

skill noun

*Everyone admired her **skill** at sudoku.*

ability
talent
expertise

skin noun

1 *Their clothes were made of animal **skins**.*

a hide
a fur
a pelt

2 *You can eat the **skin** of some fruits.*

the rind
the peel

skip verb

1 *She **skipped** happily down the road.*

to dance
to prance
to trip
to trot

2 *The lambs **skipped** about in the fields.*

to jump
to leap
to frisk
to prance

sledge noun

*The children were playing on **sledges**.*

a toboggan
a sleigh a sledge that is pulled by animals

sleep verb sleeps, sleeping, slept

1 *He was **sleeping** in front of the fire.*

to be asleep
to fall asleep
to doze
to snooze
to slumber

to snore
to have a nap
to nod off

2 *Some animals **sleep** all winter.*

to hibernate

sleepy adjective

*I was **sleepy** so I went to bed.*

tired
drowsy
weary
OPPOSITE wide awake

slept verb past tense *see* sleep

slid verb past tense *see* slide

slide verb slides, sliding, slid

1 *The sledge **slid** across the ice.*

to glide
to skim
to slither

2 *The car **slid** on the icy road.*

to skid
to slip

slight adjective

*We've got a **slight** problem.*

small
little
minor
unimportant

slim adjective

*She was tall and **slim**.*

thin

slender

slip verb

1 *Sam **slipped** and fell over.*

to trip

to stumble

to lose your balance *He **lost his balance**.*

2 *The wheels kept **slipping** on the wet road.*

to slide

to skid

slippery adjective

*Take care: the floor is **slippery**.*

slippy

greasy

oily

slimy

icy

slithery

slope noun

*We climbed up the steep **slope** to the castle.*

a hill

a bank

a rise

slope verb

1 *The beach **slopes** down to the sea.*

to drop

to dip

to fall

2 *The field **slopes** gently upwards.*

to rise

3 *The floor **slopes** to one side.*

to tilt

to slant

to lean

sloppy adjective

1 *The cake mixture was too **sloppy**.*

wet

runny

watery

2 *This is a very **sloppy** piece of work and you will have to do it again!*

careless

messy

untidy

shoddy

slow adjective

1 *They were walking at a **slow** pace.*

steady

leisurely

unhurried

dawdling

2 *We got stuck behind a **slow** lorry on the main road.*

slow-moving

3 *He made a **slow** recovery from his illness.*

steady

gradual

OPPOSITE quick

sly adjective

*They say the fox is a **sly** animal.*

clever

crafty

cunning

wily

devious

smack verb

*Don't **smack**! It is not very nice.*

to slap

to hit

to spank

a
b
c
d
e
f
g
h
i
j
k
l
m
n
o
p
q
r
s
t
u
v
w
x
y
z

A
B
C
D
E
F
G
H
I
J
K
L
M
N
O
P
Q
R
S
T
U
V
W
X
Y
Z

small adjective

OVERUSED WORD

Here are some more interesting words for **small**:

1 *He handed me a **small** box.*
little
Use **tiny**, **titchy**, or **minute** for something that is very small:
*She was riding a strange-looking bike with **tiny** wheels.*

2 *They live in a **small** flat.*
little
tiny
Use **cramped** or **poky** for a room or building that is too small: *Our classroom would feel very **cramped** with 50 children in it.*

3 *I'm quite **small** for my age.*
short
slight
petite

4 *She gave us **small** helpings.*
mean
measly
stingy

5 *These clothes are too **small** for me.*
tight
short

6 *It's only a **small** problem.*
little
slight
minor
OPPOSITE **big**

smart adjective

1 *You look very **smart** in your new clothes.*
neat
elegant
stylish
well-dressed
chic
OPPOSITE **scruffy**

2 *He's a **smart** boy.*
clever
intelligent
bright
sharp
OPPOSITE **stupid**

smear verb

*The baby had **smeared** jam all over the walls and made a terrible mess.*
to wipe
to rub
to spread
to daub

smell noun

*What's that **smell**?*

A **scent**, **perfume**, or **fragrance** is a nice smell, like the smell of perfume or flowers: *These roses have a lovely **scent**.*

An **aroma** is a nice smell of food cooking: *A delicious **aroma** of fresh bread was coming from the kitchen.*

A **stink**, **stench**, or **odour** is a nasty smell: *There was a horrible **stink** of sweaty socks!*

smell verb

*Your feet **smell**!*
to stink
to reek
to pong

smile verb

*She looked up and **smiled** at me.*

Use **grin** or **beam** when someone smiles because they are happy: *The children **beamed** when they saw the presents.*

Use **smirk** when someone smiles in an annoying way: *Henry **smirked** at me when I got told off.*

smooth adjective

1 *Roll out the dough on a **smooth** surface.*

level

even

flat

OPPOSITE **uneven**

2 *I stroked the cat's lovely **smooth** fur.*

soft

silky

velvety

sleek

OPPOSITE **rough**

3 *We rowed across the **smooth** surface of the lake.*

calm

flat

still

OPPOSITE **rough**

snatch verb

*The dog **snatched** the sandwich off me.*

to grab

to take

to pull

to seize

sneak verb

*She **sneaked** out of the room.*

to creep

to slip

to steal

soft adjective

1 *Work the clay with your hands until it is **soft**.*

doughy

squashy

malleable

OPPOSITE **hard**

2 *The bed was warm and **soft**.*

springy

OPPOSITE **hard**

3 *The kitten's coat was lovely and **soft**.*

smooth

fluffy

furry

silky

velvety

OPPOSITE **rough**

4 *Our feet sank into the **soft** ground.*

boggy

marshy

spongy

squashy

OPPOSITE **hard**

5 ***Soft** music played in the background.*

quiet

gentle

low

soothing

restful

OPPOSITE **loud**

a
b
c
d
e
f
g
h
i
j
k
l
m
n
o
p
q
r
s
t
u
v
w
x
y
z

177

A
B
C
D
E
F
G
H
I
J
K
L
M
N
O
P
Q
R
S
T
U
V
W
X
Y
Z

soldier noun

*They have sent **soldiers** to fight the terrorists.*
troops *They have sent **troops**.*
the army *They have sent the **army**.*

solid adjective

1 *The walls are **solid**.*
dense
rigid
strong
OPPOSITE **hollow**
2 *Water becomes **solid** when it freezes.*
hard
firm
OPPOSITE **soft**

solve verb

*Have you **solved** the mystery yet?*
to work out
to figure out
to get to the bottom of

song noun

*As he walked along he sang a little **song**.*
a tune
a ditty

WORD WEB

Some types of **song**:

an anthem
a ballad
a carol
  a Christmas song
a folk song
a hymn a religious song

a lullaby a song to send a baby to sleep
a melody
a nursery rhyme
a pop song
a rap

---

sore adjective

*My knee is **sore**.*
hurting
painful
Use **aching** if something is sore for a long time: *I sat down to rest my **aching** feet.*

Use **throbbing** if something is sore with a banging pain: *My knee was still **throbbing** the next morning.*

Use **bruised** if something has a bruise on it: *Mum gently bathed my **bruised** knee.*

Use **tender** if something is sore when you touch it: *I can walk around now, but my leg is still a bit **tender**.*

sorry adjective

1 *He was **sorry** when he saw the damage he had done.*
apologetic
ashamed
upset
remorseful
OPPOSITE **unrepentant**
2 *I feel **sorry** for the little girl.*
sympathetic *I feel **sympathetic** towards the little girl.*
OPPOSITE **unsympathetic**

sort noun

1 *What **sort** of sandwich do you want?*
a type
a kind
a variety
2 *A terrier is a **sort** of dog.*
a breed
3 *A ladybird is a **sort** of beetle.*
a species

4 *What* **sort** *of trainers do you want to buy?*

a brand

a make

sort verb

We **sorted** *the books into three different piles.*

to arrange

to group

to organize

sound noun

I heard a strange **sound** *coming from the kitchen.*

a noise

sour adjective

Lemon has a **sour** *taste.*

bitter

sharp

acid

tart

OPPOSITE sweet

space noun

1 *Is there enough* **space** *for me there as well?*

room

WORD WEB

Some loud **sounds**:

bang	**rattle**
boom	**ring**
buzz	**roar**
clang	**rumble**
clank	**thud**
clatter	**thump**
crash	**whistle**
pop	

Some gentle **sounds**:

bleep	**fizz**	**splash**
click	**hum**	**tick**
drip	**plop**	**whirr**

a
b
c
d
e
f
g
h
i
j
k
l
m
n
o
p
q
r
s
t
u
v
w
x
y
z

A B C D E F G H I J K L M N O P Q R **S** T U V W X Y Z

2 *We squeezed through a* **space** *between the two rocks.*
a gap
a hole
an opening

spacecraft noun
I would love to go in a **spacecraft***.*
a spaceship
a rocket
a space shuttle

spare adjective
Remember to take a **spare** *pair of shoes.*
extra
additional

sparkle verb
The sea **sparkled** *in the sunlight.*
to shine
to glisten
to shimmer
to glint

speak verb speaks, speaking, spoke
Everyone started to **speak** *at once.*
to talk
to say something
to chatter
to start a conversation

special adjective
1 *Your birthday is a very* **special** *day.*
important
significant
unusual
extraordinary

2 *I've got my own* **special** *mug.*
personal
individual
particular
OPPOSITE ordinary

spectacular adjective
We watched a **spectacular** *fireworks display.*
exciting
impressive
magnificent
wonderful
grand
amazing

sped verb past tense see speed

speed noun
1 *We were walking at a fairly average* **speed***.*
a pace
2 *The pilot told us the height and* **speed** *of the aeroplane.*
velocity
3 *They worked with amazing* **speed***.*
quickness
swiftness
haste

speed verb speeds, speeding, sped
A sports car **sped** *past us.*
to shoot
to zoom
to whizz
to flash

spell noun
She was under a magic **spell***.*
an enchantment
a charm
a bewitchment

spend verb spends, spending, spent
I've already spent all my pocket money.

to use

to pay out *I paid out a lot of money for that jacket.*

spent past tense *see* **spend**

spill verb spills, spilling, spilled or spilt
1 *Mind you don't spill your drink.*

to drop

to knock over

to upset

2 *She spilt milk all over the kitchen floor.*

to drop

to pour

to tip

to slop

3 *Some water had spilt on to the floor.*

to drip

to leak

to splash

4 *Water was spilling over the edge of the bath.*

to pour

to run

to stream

to gush

to splash

spin verb spins, spinning, spun
1 *I span round when I heard his voice.*

to turn

to whirl

to swivel

2 *The dancers spun across the floor.*

to twirl

to pirouette

3 *The back wheel of my bike was still spinning.*

to turn

to revolve

to rotate

to go round

spiteful adjective
It wasn't nice to say those spiteful things about your friend.

nasty

unkind

horrible

mean

OPPOSITE **kind**

splash verb
1 *They splashed us with water and we were soaking.*

to shower

to spray

to squirt

to spatter

2 *They splashed water all over the floor.*

to spill

to slop

to slosh

split verb splits, splitting, split
1 *He split the log with an axe.*

to cut

to chop

2 *The bag split open and oranges fell out.*

to break

to tear

to rip

3 *We split the sandwich between us.*

to share

to divide

a
b
c
d
e
f
g
h
i
j
k
l
m
n
o
p
q
r
s
t
u
v
w
x
y
z

A
B
C
D
E
F
G
H
I
J
K
L
M
N
O
P
Q
R
S
T
U
V
W
X
Y
Z

spoil verb
1 *The water had **spoilt** some of the books.*
to damage
to ruin
2 *The bad weather **spoilt** our holiday.*
to ruin
to mess up

spoke verb past tense *see* **speak**

sport noun
*Do you enjoy **sport**?*
exercise
games

spot noun
1 *Leopards have dark **spots** on their bodies.*
a mark
a dot
a blotch
a patch
2 *Oh, no! I've got a **spot** on my nose!*
a pimple
Acne is a lot of spots on your face: *Some teenagers get very bad **acne**.*

A rash is a lot of spots you get when you are ill: *Chickenpox gives you a **rash**.*

3 *There were a few **spots** of paint on the door.*
a mark
a dot
a drop
a blob
a smear
a smudge
4 *We found a lovely **spot** for a picnic.*
a place
a site
a location

WORD WEB

*Some team **sports**:*
baseball
basketball
cricket
football
hockey
ice hockey
netball
rounders
rugby
volleyball

*Some individual **sports**:*
athletics
badminton
canoeing
cycling
fishing
golf
gymnastics
ice skating
jogging
judo
karate
kick-boxing
skiing
snooker
snowboarding
swimming
table tennis
tae kwondo
tennis
trampolining

diving

snowboarding

cycling

kick-boxing

gymnastics

running

football

canoeing

a
b
c
d
e
f
g
h
i
j
k
l
m
n
o
p
q
r
s
t
u
v
w
x
y
z

183

A
B
C
D
E
F
G
H
I
J
K
L
M
N
O
P
Q
R
S
T
U
V
W
X
Y
Z

spray verb

1 *He **sprayed** some water on to the plants.*

to splash
to sprinkle
to squirt

2 *She **sprayed** us with water.*

to splash
to shower
to squirt

spread verb spreads, spreading, spread

1 *The bird **spread** its wings and flew away.*

to open
to stretch out

2 *We **spread** a cloth on the ground.*

to lay out
to unfold
to open out
to arrange

3 *I **spread** some jam on to the bread.*

to put
to smear

spun verb past tense see spin

squabble verb

*My brothers are always **squabbling**.*

to argue
to quarrel
to disagree
to fall out
to fight
to bicker

squash verb

1 *Mind you don't **squash** those flowers.*

to crush
to flatten

to damage
to break

2 *We all **squashed** into the back of the car.*

to squeeze
to crowd

3 *I **squashed** everything into the suitcase.*

to push
to shove
to cram
to squeeze
to jam

squeeze verb

1 *We all **squeezed** into the tiny room.*

to squash
to crowd

2 *I **squeezed** everything into my bag.*

to push
to shove
to squash
to cram
to jam

squirt verb

1 *Water **squirted** out of the hole.*

to spurt
to gush
to spray

2 *She **squirted** water at me.*

to spray
to splash

stage noun

*We have finished the first **stage** of our journey.*

a part
a phase

stain noun

Her shirt was covered in stains from cooking.

a mark

a spot

a smudge

a smear

stale adjective

All we had to eat was water and stale bread.

old

dry

mouldy

OPPOSITE fresh

stand verb stands, standing, stood

1 *We all stood when the visitors arrived.*

to get up

to get to your feet *We all got to our feet.*

to rise *We all rose.*

2 *I can't stand this noise!*

to bear

to put up with

to tolerate

standard noun

The standard of your work has improved.

level

quality

stare verb

Why is everyone staring at me?

to look

to gaze

Use **gape** if you stare at someone in a surprised way: *My friends all gaped at me as I climbed onto the horse.*

Use **glare** if you stare at someone in an angry way: *My aunt glared at me angrily, so I knew I had to behave.*

start verb

1 *What time does the programme start?*

to begin

to commence

OPPOSITE finish

2 *We're going to start a running club.*

to set up

to create

to establish

3 *She started the engine.*

to switch on

to turn on

start noun

When is the start of the hockey season?

the beginning

OPPOSITE end

stay verb

1 *Stay here until I come back.*

to remain

to wait

to hang around

2 *Stay on this path until you reach the river.*

to continue

to carry on

3 *I'm going to stay with my grandma.*

to visit

4 *I hope it stays dry this afternoon.*

to remain

steady adjective

1 *Make sure the ladder is steady so you don't fall off.*

firm

stable

secure

balanced

OPPOSITE wobbly

a b c d e f g h i j k l m n o p q r **s** t u v w x y z

185

A
B
C
D
E
F
G
H
I
J
K
L
M
N
O
P
Q
R
S
T
U
V
W
X
Y
Z

2 *The music had a **steady** rhythm.*
even
regular
constant
OPPOSITE **irregular**

steal verb steals, stealing, stole
*Someone's **stolen** my purse.*
to take
to pinch
to nick

steep adjective
*There was a **steep** drop down to the river.*
sharp
vertical
sheer
OPPOSITE **gradual**

step noun
1 *He took a **step** forwards.*
a pace
a stride
2 *I climbed up the **steps**.*
stairs

stick noun
1 *We collected some **sticks** to make a fire.*
a twig
a branch
2 *He was holding a long **stick**.*
a pole
a rod
a cane
A **baton** is a stick you use to conduct an orchestra, or in a relay race.
A **truncheon** is a stick that a policeman carries.
A **club** is a stick you use as a weapon.
A **walking stick** or **crutch** is a stick you use to help you walk.

stick verb sticks, sticking, stuck
1 *I **stuck** the pictures in my book.*
to glue
to fix
to paste
2 *Sometimes the door **sticks** a bit.*
to jam
to get stuck
3 *She **stuck** a pin into my arm.*
to jab
to stab
to pierce

sticky adjective
*She picked up some of the **sticky** mixture.*
gooey
tacky
gluey
gummy

stiff adjective
1 *Use a piece of **stiff** cardboard for the base of the model.*
hard
rigid
OPPOSITE **soft**
2 *Mix the ingredients together to make a **stiff** paste.*
thick
firm
OPPOSITE **soft**
3 *The door handle was a bit **stiff**.*
stuck
jammed
difficult to move
4 *I woke up with a **stiff** neck.*
sore
painful

still adjective

1 *It was a very **still** evening.*

quiet

calm

peaceful

2 *We all stood perfectly **still**.*

motionless

stir verb

*She **stirred** the mixture with a spoon.*

to mix

to beat

to whisk

stole verb past tense *see* **steal**

stone noun

*He threw a **stone** into the water.*

A **pebble** is a small, round stone: *We found some pretty **pebbles** on the beach.*

A **rock** is a big stone: *We climbed over the **rocks** and down to the sea.*

A **boulder** is a very big heavy stone: *Huge **boulders** came tumbling down the mountainside.*

stood verb past tense *see* **stand**

stop verb

1 *The policeman **stopped** the traffic.*

to halt

to hold up

2 *The bus **stopped** outside the school.*

to pull up

to draw up

to park

to come to a halt

to grind to a halt

to come to a standstill

3 *He **stopped** for a moment.*

to hesitate

to pause

to wait

4 *Shall we **stop** for lunch?*

to break off

to knock off

5 *I wish you would **stop** teasing your brother!*

to finish

to quit

to give up

6 *This silly behaviour has got to **stop**.*

to end

to finish

to come to an end

to cease

7 *It is time to **stop** this nonsense.*

to end

to put an end to

to put a stop to

8 *We must **stop** him from getting away.*

to prevent

storm noun

*That night there was a terrible **storm** and we were glad to be inside the house.*

A **thunderstorm** is a storm with thunder.
A **blizzard** is a storm with snow: *The **blizzard** had left huge snowdrifts the next morning.*

A **gale**, **hurricane**, or **tornado is** a storm with a very strong wind: *A lot of buildings were damaged by the **hurricane**.*

a
b
c
d
e
f
g
h
i
j
k
l
m
n
o
p
q
r
s
t
u
v
w
x
y
z

A
B
C
D
E
F
G
H
I
J
K
L
M
N
O
P
Q
R
S
T
U
V
W
X
Y
Z

story noun

*He told us a **story** about a fox.*

a tale

a yarn

WORD WEB

*Some types of **story**:*

an adventure story

a fable

a fairy tale

a fantasy story

a folk tale

a legend

a myth

a parable

a science fiction story

a traditional tale

straight adjective

*That picture isn't **straight**.*

level

upright

OPPOSITE **crooked**

strain verb

1 *I had to **strain** to reach the handle.*

to struggle

to try hard

to make an effort

2 *I **strained** a muscle when I was running.*

to hurt

to injure

to damage

strange adjective

1 *What a **strange** animal the sloth is!*

funny

peculiar

odd

curious

unusual

extraordinary

remarkable

OPPOSITE **normal**

2 *When I woke up I was in a **strange** place.*

different

new

unfamiliar

unknown

OPPOSITE **familiar**

street noun

*That boy lives in the same **street** as me.*

a road

an avenue

a crescent

strength noun

*I had to use all my **strength** to open the door.*

force

might

power

energy

force

stretch verb

*You can **stretch** elastic.*

to pull out

to lengthen

to extend

to tighten

strict adjective

*Our teacher is quite **strict**.*

harsh

severe

stern

firm

rigid

string noun

*We tied the parcel up with **string**.*

cord
rope
twine
ribbon

stripe noun

*She was wearing a blue dress with white **stripes**.*

a line
a band

strong adjective

struggle verb

1 *The thief **struggled** to get away.*

to fight
to wrestle

2 *We were **struggling** to carry all the boxes.*

to try hard
to work hard

stubborn adjective

*He was **stubborn** and refused to leave her.*

obstinate
defiant
wilful
pig-headed

OVERUSED WORD

Here are some more interesting words for **strong**:

1 *He is **strong** enough to be a weightlifter.*

tough
powerful

Use **muscular**, **brawny**, or **strapping** for someone who has big muscles: *The lifeguard was tall and **muscular**.*

2 *She has been very ill, and she is not **strong** enough to go outside yet.*

well
fit
healthy

3 *The rope wasn't **strong** enough to hold my weight.*

tough
thick

4 *The roof must be made of a **strong** material.*

tough
solid
hard-wearing
heavy-duty
durable
unbreakable
indestructible

5 *The shelter they had built was quite **strong**.*

well-made
well-built
sturdy

6 *This orange squash is too **strong**.*

concentrated

OPPOSITE weak

A
B
C
D
E
F
G
H
I
J
K
L
M
N
O
P
Q
R
S
T
U
V
W
X
Y
Z

stuck verb past tense *see* **stick**

study verb
1 *We're* **studying** *the Romans at school.*
to learn about
to read about
to research
to investigate
2 *He* **studied** *the map carefully.*
to look at
to examine

stuff noun
1 *There was some sticky* **stuff** *on the floor.*
a substance *There was a sticky* **substance** *on the floor.*

2 *We cleared all the old* **stuff** *out of the cupboards.*
things
odds and ends
bits and pieces
3 *Don't forget to take all your* **stuff** *with you.*
things
belongings
possessions
kit

stumble verb
I **stumbled** *over a big stone.*
to trip
to slip
to lose your balance

stupid adjective
1 *That was a* **stupid** *thing to do!*
silly
daft *(informal)*
foolish
unwise
idiotic
2 *You must be* **stupid** *if you believe that!*
daft
dim
dense
brainless
thick *(informal)*
OPPOSITE **intelligent**

subtract verb
Can you **subtract** *6 from 9?*
to take away
to deduct
to find the difference between *Can you* **find the difference between** *6 and 9?*

succeed verb
1 *I know she will* **succeed** *in becoming a pilot.*
to manage
to be successful
2 *All children should try to* **succeed** *at school.*
to do well
3 *Did your plan* **succeed***?*
to work
to be successful *Was your plan* **successful***?*
OPPOSITE **fail**

success noun

*The concert was a great **success**.*

a triumph

a hit

OPPOSITE failure

sudden adjective

1 *There was a **sudden** change in the weather.*

unexpected

abrupt

2 *He made a **sudden** dash for the door.*

quick

swift

hasty

hurried

suggest verb

*I **suggested** that we should go back home.*

to propose

to advise

to recommend

suggestion noun

*What do you think we should do? What's your **suggestion**?*

an idea

a proposal

a plan

suit verb

*That dress really **suits** you.*

to look nice on *That dress looks nice on you.*

to look right on *That dress looks right on you.*

sulky adjective

*He's been **sulky** all afternoon.*

moody

sullen

bad-tempered

grumpy

sunny adjective

*It was a lovely **sunny** day.*

bright

fine

clear

cloudless

summery

OPPOSITE cloudy

supply noun

*There's a **supply** of coloured paper in the cupboard.*

a store

a stock

a reserve

a source

a hoard

support verb

1 *Those four pillars are **supporting** the gymnasium roof.*

to hold up

to prop up

to reinforce

to bear

2 *You should **support** your friends when they are in trouble.*

to help

to defend

to stand up for

to stick up for

3 *Samir and Ben went to **support** their team last Saturday.*

to encourage

to cheer on

suppose verb

1 *I suppose we ought to go home now.*
to think
to guess
to reckon
2 *I suppose she must be the new teacher.*
to assume
to presume

sure adjective

1 *I'm sure she lives somewhere round here.*
certain
positive
convinced
confident
2 *He's sure to remember.*
bound
OPPOSITE **unsure**

surprise noun

1 *Winning the competition was a complete surprise.*
a shock
a bombshell
a bolt from the blue
2 *He looked at me in surprise.*
amazement
astonishment
wonder

surprise verb

It surprised everyone when our team won the game.
to amaze
to astonish
to astound
to shock
to startle
to stagger

surprised adjective

I was surprised when I saw all the presents.
amazed
astonished
astounded
staggered
flabbergasted *(informal)*
shocked

surrender verb

After a long game, the team surrendered.
to give in
to capitulate
to yield

survive verb

The plane crashed, but all the passengers survived.
to live
to stay alive

suspect verb

I suspect that he is not telling the truth.
to think
to believe
to guess
to have a feeling *I have a feeling that he is not telling the truth.*
to have a hunch *I have a hunch that he is not telling the truth.*

swam verb past tense *see* swim

swear verb swears, swearing, swore

1 *He swore he would not forget PE kit.*
to promise
to vow
to give your word *He gave his word that he would never do it again.*

2 *The teacher told him off because he* **swore**.
to use bad language
to curse

sweet adjective

1 *This orange juice is too* **sweet**.
sugary
OPPOSITE **bitter**
2 *That little dog is really* **sweet**!
lovely
lovable
cute
adorable
OPPOSITE **ugly**

swim verb swims, swimming, swam

We **swam** *in the river.*
to bathe
to go swimming

swing verb swings, swinging, swung

1 *The loose rope was* **swinging** *backwards and forwards.*
to sway
to wave
2 *The monkey was* **swinging** *energetically from a branch.*
to hang
to dangle

switch noun

Don't touch any of those **switches**.
a button
a knob
a control

switch verb

I **switched** *the light on.*
to turn

swoop verb

The owl **swooped** *down on its prey.*
to dive
to drop
to descend *The owl* **descended** *on its prey.*

swore verb past tense *see* swear

swung verb past tense *see* swing

sympathy noun

Everyone gave me a lot of **sympathy** *when I was ill.*
compassion
understanding
pity

Tt

take verb takes, taking, took

1 *I offered him a sandwich and he **took** one.*
to pick up
to take hold of
Use **grab**, **snatch**, or **grasp** if someone takes something roughly: *Sara rudely **snatched** the book out of my hands.*

2 *Don't forget to **take** your lunch.*
to carry
to bring

3 *The nurse **took** us to the ward.*
to lead
to accompany
to guide

4 *Dad **took** us to the station in his car.*
to drive
to transport
to give someone a lift *Dad **gave us a lift** in his car.*

5 *The burglar **took** the jewels.*
to steal
to pinch
to seize
to run off with

take out
*The dentist **took** out one of my teeth.*
to remove
to pull out
to extract

talent noun
*He's a tennis player with a lot of **talent**.*
ability
skill
flair
aptitude

talented adjective
*He is a very **talented** juggler.*
clever
gifted
skilful
able

talk noun
1 *I had a **talk** with my teacher.*
a chat
a conversation
a discussion
2 *Mr Rose gave us a **talk** on owls.*
a speech
a lecture

talk verb
1 *We **talked** about our hobbies.*
to chat
to converse
to have a conversation
to have a discussion
2 *The teacher told us to stop **talking**.*
to chat
to chatter
to natter
to gossip

A B C D E F G H I J K L M N O P Q R S **T** U V W X Y Z

tall adjective

1 *She is quite **tall** for her age.*

big

lanky

OPPOSITE **short**

2 *There are some **tall** buildings in the city.*

big

high

lofty

towering

OPPOSITE **low**

tame adjective

*The animals in the farm are all very **tame**.*

gentle

docile

safe

obedient

OPPOSITE **wild**

tangled adjective

*The string was all **tangled**.*

knotted

twisted

tap verb

*She **tapped** quietly on the door.*

to knock

to rap

taste noun

1 *The ice cream had a lovely creamy **taste**.*

a flavour

2 *Can I have a **taste** of your chocolate?*

a bit

a bite

a piece

a mouthful

a nibble

3 *He let me have a **taste** of his orange juice.*

a sip

a mouthful

taste verb

*Would you like to **taste** my drink?*

to try

to sample

taught verb past tense *see* **teach**

teach verb teaches, teaching, taught

1 *A teacher's job is to **teach** children.*

to educate

2 *My brother **taught** me how to use the computer.*

to show

to tell

to train *He **trained** us to use the computer.*

tear verb tears, tearing, tore

*Be careful you don't **tear** your dress.*

to rip

to split

tease verb

*Sometimes my friends **tease** me about my hair.*

to make fun of

to laugh at

to torment

to taunt

telephone verb

*I'll **telephone** you later.*

to phone

to call

to ring

to give someone a ring *(informal)*

*I'll **give you a ring** later.*

a b c d e f g h i j k l m n o p q r s **t** u v w x y z

A
B
C
D
E
F
G
H
I
J
K
L
M
N
O
P
Q
R
S
T
U
V
W
X
Y
Z

tell verb tells, telling, told

1 *He* **told** *me he'd be home for tea.*

to say *He said he'd be home for tea.*

to promise *He promised he'd be home for tea.*

2 *My dad* **told** *me how to use a calculator.*

to show

to teach

to explain *He explained to me how to use a calculator.*

3 *You should* **tell** *the police if you see anything unusual.*

to inform

to notify

4 *She finally* **told** *me the secret.*

to reveal *She revealed the secret to me.*

5 *My dad* **told** *us a story.*

to relate *He related a story.*

to narrate *He narrated a story to us.*

6 *Can you* **tell** *us what happened?*

to describe *Can you describe what happened?*

to recount *Can you recount what happened?*

7 *Mum* **told** *us to stop shouting.*

to order

to instruct

to command

tell off

The teacher **told** *us* **off** *for talking during class.*

to scold

to reprimand

to rebuke

temper noun

1 *You seem to be in a very good* **temper** *today.*

mood

humour

2 *The man was in a horrible* **temper***!*

a rage

a fury

terrible adjective

1 *The weather was* **terrible***!*

awful

dreadful

appalling

horrible

ghastly

2 *This is* **terrible** *news!*

bad

sad

awful

shocking

upsetting

3 *I'm a* **terrible** *tennis player.*

hopeless

useless

terrific adjective

I think that's a **terrific** *idea!*

wonderful

brilliant

excellent

fantastic

terrify verb

I am **terrified** *of singing in front of people.*

to frighten

to scare

to petrify

terror noun

People ran away from the fire in **terror***.*

fear

fright

panic

test noun

*We've got a spelling **test** tomorrow.*

an exam

an examination

test verb

*Now we must **test** the machine to see if it works.*

to try

to try out

to use

thank verb

*I **thanked** them for their present.*

to say thank you

to express your gratitude *I expressed my gratitude.*

to show your appreciation *I showed my appreciation.*

thaw verb

1 *The snow has started to **thaw**.*

to melt

2 *I took the meat out of the freezer so that it would **thaw**.*

to defrost

to warm up

thick adjective

1 *He drew a **thick** line.*

wide

broad

2 *The castle had **thick** stone walls.*

solid

strong

3 *She cut herself a **thick** slice of cake.*

big

large

fat

4 *We had to walk through **thick** mud.*

deep

5 *He was wearing a **thick** coat.*

heavy

warm

OPPOSITE **thin**

thief noun

*The money was stolen by a **thief**.*

a robber

A **burglar** goes into a person's house to steal things: *Always lock your windows so that **burglars** can't get in.*

A **pickpocket** steals things from a person's pocket: *Be careful, there are **pickpockets** about on the streets.*

A **mugger** attacks someone in the street and steals things from them: *The man was attacked by a **mugger**.*

A **shoplifter** steals things from shops: *There are security men to catch **shoplifters**.*

thin adjective

1 *She drew a **thin** line across the page.*

fine

narrow

OPPOSITE **thick**

2 *The dog we rescued is very **thin**.*

slim

slender

Use **skinny**, **scrawny**, or **bony** for someone who is too thin: *The evil witch had horrible **bony** hands.*

OPPOSITE **fat**

3 *This paint is too **thin**.*

watery

weak

runny

diluted

OPPOSITE **thick**

a b c d e f g h i j k l m n o p q r s **t** u v w x y z

197

4 *She was only wearing a* **thin** *cotton dress.*
light
flimsy
OPPOSITE **thick**

thing noun
1 *We found some very interesting* **things** *in the attic.*
an object
an article
an item
2 *Don't forget to take all your* **things** *with you when you leave.*
belongings
possessions
stuff
3 *A corkscrew is a* **thing** *for opening bottles.*
a tool
a device
a gadget
a machine
4 *A very strange* **thing** *happened to me today.*
an event
an incident
5 *We had to do some very difficult* **things.**
an action
an act
a job
a task

think verb thinks, thinking, thought
1 **Think** *before you act.*
to concentrate
to use your mind
2 *He was sitting in a chair just* **thinking.**
to meditate
to muse
to daydream

3 *I* **thought** *about what had happened.*
to reflect on *I* **reflected on** *what happened.*
to mull over *I* **mulled over** *what happened.*
to ponder *I* **pondered** *over what happened.*
4 *He was still* **thinking** *about what to do.*
to consider *He was* **considering** *what to do.*
to plan *He was* **planning** *what he would do with the money he'd been given for his birthday.*
5 *I* **think** *that you are right.*
to believe
to reckon
to suppose

thought verb
past tense *see* **think**

thought noun
I've just had an amazing **thought** *like a light bulb moment.*
an idea
a brainwave
a notion

thoughtful adjective
1 *He was sitting on his own, looking* **thoughtful.**
serious
pensive
reflective
2 *You should try to be more* **thoughtful.**
considerate
kind
caring
helpful
unselfish
OPPOSITE **thoughtless**

threw verb past tense *see* **throw**

throw verb throws, throwing, threw

1 *She* **threw** *a stone and broke the glass.*

Use **fling** or **hurl** when you throw something with a lot of force: *Someone had* **hurled** *a brick through the greenhouse window.*

Use **toss** when you throw something carelessly. **Sling** or **chuck** are informal ways of saying this too: *She* **tossed** *the letter into the bin.*

Use **lob** when you throw something high into the air: *I* **lobbed** *the ball over the fence.*

2 *He* **threw** *the ball towards the batsman.*

to bowl

throw away

My old shoes didn't fit me any more so I **threw** *them* **away**.

to throw out
to get rid of
to dispose of
to discard
to dump

tidy adjective

1 *My aunt's house is always very* **tidy**.

neat
shipshape
orderly
uncluttered
spick and span

2 *The children all looked* **tidy**.

neat
smart
well-groomed

3 *Are you a* **tidy** *person?*

neat
organized
house-proud
OPPOSITE **untidy**

tie verb

1 *I can't* **tie** *my shoelaces.*

to do up
to fasten

2 *Why don't you* **tie** *the two bits together?*

to fasten
to join
to fix
to knot

3 *They* **tied** *the boat to a post.*

to fasten
to secure
to moor

4 *He* **tied** *the animal to the fence.*

to tether

tight adjective

1 *My trousers are a bit* **tight**.

small
tight-fitting
close-fitting

2 *Make sure the jar has a* **tight** *lid.*

firm
secure

3 *Pull the rope until it is* **tight**.

stretched
taut
OPPOSITE **loose**

time noun

1 *He sat in silence for a long* **time**.

a while
a period

2 *The 1960s was a very interesting* **time** *for music.*

a period
an era
an age

a
b
c
d
e
f
g
h
i
j
k
l
m
n
o
p
q
r
s
t
u
v
w
x
y
z

A B C D E F G H I J K L M N O P Q R **S** **T** U V W X Y Z

3 *I thought this was a good **time** to ask for more pocket money.*

a moment
an opportunity

tiny adjective

*Some insects are **tiny**.*

minute
minuscule
microscopic
OPPOSITE big

tip noun

1 *She stood up on the **tips** of her toes.*

the end
the point

2 *We could only see the **tip** of the iceberg.*

the top

tip verb

1 *I could feel the bench beginning to **tip** back.*

to lean
to tilt

2 *She **tipped** water all over the floor.*

to pour
to spill
to slop

tip over

*The boat **tipped over** in the rough sea.*

to capsize
to overturn

tired adjective

1 *We were **tired** after our walk.*

weary

Use **exhausted** or **worn out** when you are very tired: *I was **exhausted** after our long day.*

Use **sleepy** when you are tired and want to sleep: *This warm fire is making me **sleepy**.*

2 *I'm tired of this game.*

fed up *I'm **fed up** with this game.*
bored *I'm **bored** with this game.*

told verb past tense *see* tell

took verb past tense *see* take

tool noun

*You can use a special **tool** to get the lid off.*

a device
a gadget
an implement

WORD WEB

Some **tools** for woodwork:

a drill
a hammer
a plane
pliers
a screwdriver
a spanner

Some **tools** you use in the garden:

a fork
a hoe
a rake
shears
a spade
a trowel
a watering can

a screwdriver

---

top noun

1 *We climbed to the **top** of the mountain.*

the summit

2 *We could see the **tops** of the mountains in the distance.*

a peak
a tip

3 *We drove over the **top** of the hill.*

the crest

4 *Put the* **top** *back on the jar.*
a lid
a cover
a cap
OPPOSITE **bottom**

tore verb *past tense see* **tear**

torment verb
Stop **tormenting** *each other!*
to tease
to bully
to annoy

total adjective
1 *What will the* **total** *cost be?*
full
whole
2 *Because it rained, the picnic was a* **total** *disaster.*
complete
absolute

touch verb
1 *He* **touched** *my arm lightly.*
to pat
to tap
to stroke
to brush
2 *You mustn't* **touch** *the things on display in the museum.*
to handle
to hold
to feel
3 *Please don't* **touch** *the controls.*
to fiddle with
to mess about with *(informal)*
to play with

tough adjective
1 *The rope is made of very* **tough** *nylon.*
strong
hard-wearing
unbreakable
2 *He thinks he's a really* **tough** *guy.*
strong
hard
rough
violent
OPPOSITE **weak**

traffic noun
There was a lot of **traffic** *on the road.*
cars
lorries
buses
coaches
vans
vehicles

tragedy noun
The plane crash was a terrible **tragedy**.
a disaster
a catastrophe
a calamity

train verb
1 *Mr Grout* **trains** *our swimming team.*
to coach
to instruct
to teach
2 *Our team* **trains** *every Thursday.*
to practise

trap verb
We **trapped** *the smugglers in the cave.*
to catch
to corner

a
b
c
d
e
f
g
h
i
j
k
l
m
n
o
p
q
r
s
t
u
v
w
x
y
z

A
B
C
D
E
F
G
H
I
J
K
L
M
N
O
P
Q
R
S
T
U
V
W
X
Y
Z

travel verb

*We **travelled** all around the world.*

to go
to journey
to tour
to drive
to sail
to fly
to walk
to ride
to cycle
to hitch-hike

treasure noun

*We found a box of buried **treasure**.*

gold
silver
jewels
riches

tree noun

tremble verb

*I was **trembling** with fear.*

to shake
to quake
to quiver
to shiver
to shudder

tremendous adjective

1 *The machines make a **tremendous** noise.*

great
huge
terrific

2 *We had a **tremendous** time at the pantomime.*

great
wonderful
fantastic
excellent

WORD WEB

Some types of deciduous tree:
ash
beech
birch
elm
hawthorn
hazel
horse chestnut
larch
maple
oak

poplar
sycamore
willow

Some types of evergreen tree:
fir
holly
palm
pine
yew

*Some types of **trees** around the world:*
baobab
buffalo thorn
jacaranda
mango
marula
mopane
palm

an oak

a fir

a baobab

a palm

trick noun

*1 We played a **trick** on our friends.*

a joke

a prank

a hoax

*2 The dolphins did some amazing **tricks**.*

a stunt

trick verb

*He **tricked** us into giving him our money.*

to cheat

to fool

to deceive

to swindle

to con

trickle verb

*Water **trickled** slowly out of the tap.*

to drip

to dribble

to leak

to seep

trip noun

*We went on a **trip** to the seaside.*

an outing

an excursion

a journey

a visit

a day out

trip verb

*I **tripped** on the step and fell.*

to stumble

to slip

to lose your balance *I lost my balance.*

trouble noun

*1 We have had a lot of **troubles** recently.*

difficulties

problems

cares

worries

suffering

*2 There was some **trouble** in the playground at lunchtime.*

bother

fighting

hassle

true adjective

*1 The book is based on a **true** story.*

real

genuine

actual

*2 What he said isn't **true**.*

correct

accurate

right

OPPOSITE made-up

trust verb

*Can I **trust** you to behave while I am away?*

to rely on

to depend on

to count on

try verb

*1 I **tried** to climb over the wall.*

to attempt

to make an effort

*2 Can I **try** the cake?*

to taste

to sample

*3 Would you like to **try** my new bike?*

to try out

to test

to have a go *(informal) Would you like to **have a go** on my new bike?*

a
b
c
d
e
f
g
h
i
j
k
l
m
n
o
p
q
r
s
t
u
v
w
x
y
z

A B C D E F G H I J K L M N O P Q R S **T** U V W X Y Z

tunnel noun

*There is a secret **tunnel** leading to the castle.*

a passage

an underpass a tunnel under a road

turn verb

1 *I **turned** round to see who was behind me.*

to spin

to whirl

to swivel

2 *I **turned** the key in the lock.*

to rotate

3 *The wheel began to **turn**.*

to revolve

to rotate

to spin

4 *In the autumn some leaves **turn** red.*

to become

to go

5 *Tadpoles **turn** into frogs.*

to become

to change into

6 *I **turned** the light on.*

to switch

7 *We **turned** the attic into a playroom.*

to change

to convert

to transform

turn noun

*Be patient—it will be your **turn** in a minute.*

a go

a chance

an opportunity

twinkle verb

*The lights **twinkled** in the distance.*

to shine

to sparkle

twist verb

1 *I **twisted** the wire around the pole.*

to wind

to loop

to coil

2 *She **twisted** the ribbons together.*

to plait

to wind

type noun

1 *What **type** of music do you like?*

a kind

a sort

2 *A collie is a **type** of dog.*

a breed

3 *A ladybird is a **type** of beetle.*

a species

4 *I don't like that **type** of trainers.*

a brand

a make

typical adjective

*It was a **typical** winter's day.*

normal

ordinary

average

standard

OPPOSITE **unusual**

Uu

ugly adjective

1 *We screamed when we saw the **ugly** monster coming towards us.*

horrible
hideous
frightful
repulsive
grotesque

2 *Cinderella was beautiful, but her two sisters were **ugly**.*

plain
unattractive
OPPOSITE **beautiful**

understand verb understands, understanding, understood

*Do you **understand** what I'm saying?*

to follow
to grasp
to see

understood verb past tense see understand

unemployed adjective

*My aunt is **unemployed**.*

out of work
on the dole (informal)
jobless
OPPOSITE **employed**

unfair adjective

1 *It's **unfair** if she gets more sweets than me.*

wrong
unjust
unreasonable

2 *We complained that the referee's decision was **unfair**.*

biased
OPPOSITE **fair**

unfriendly adjective

*The other children were very **unfriendly**.*

unkind
nasty
hostile
rude
mean
unwelcoming
OPPOSITE **friendly**

unhappy adjective

*I was **unhappy** at my last school.*

sad
miserable
depressed
glum
dejected
down in the dumps (informal)

Use **gloomy** or **despondent** if you think something bad is going to happen: *My dad was quite **gloomy** because he thought he was going to lose his job.*

a b c d e f g h i j k l m n o p q r s t **u** v w x y z

A
B
C
D
E
F
G
H
I
J
K
L
M
N
O
P
Q
R
S
T
U
V
W
X
Y
Z

Use **upset** or **heartbroken** if something sad has happened: *I was really* **upset** *when I fell out with my friends.*

Use **fed up** if you are unhappy and bored: *Max was* **fed up** *because all his friends were away on holiday.*
OPPOSITE **happy**

unkind adjective

Jo hates to see people being **unkind** *to animals.*

horrible
nasty
mean
cruel
spiteful
OPPOSITE **kind**

unpleasant adjective

1 *He said some* **unpleasant** *things to me and I was upset.*

horrible
nasty
mean
unkind
rude
unfriendly
upsetting

2 *The meat had an* **unpleasant** *taste.*

horrible
nasty
disgusting
revolting
terrible
OPPOSITE **pleasant**

untidy adjective

1 *My bedroom is always* **untidy**.
messy
chaotic

Use **jumbled** or **muddled** if a lot of things are mixed together in an untidy way: *There was a huge* **jumbled** *pile of clothes on the floor.*

Use **scruffy** to describe someone's clothes or appearance: *Ben never looks smart—he always looks* **scruffy**!

2 *This work is very* **untidy**!
messy
careless
sloppy
OPPOSITE **tidy**

unusual adjective

It's **unusual** *to have snow in May.*
extraordinary
odd
peculiar
strange
surprising
uncommon
OPPOSITE **ordinary**

upset adjective

Sita was crying and looked very **upset**.
sad
distressed
Use **hurt** if you are upset by something unkind that someone has done: *I felt* **hurt** *that I wasn't invited to the party.*

upset verb

1 *The pictures of the war on TV* **upset** *me.*

to distress

to sadden

to frighten

to scare

to worry

2 *Some of the nasty things he said really* **upset** *me.*

to hurt

to hurt someone's feelings *Some of the things he said* **hurt my feelings**.

use verb

1 *They* **used** *machines to dig the tunnel.*

to employ

to make use of

2 *Do you know how to* **use** *this tool?*

to handle

to manipulate

3 *He taught me how to* **use** *the machine.*

to work

to operate

4 *Have we* **used** *all the paint?*

to finish

useful adjective

1 *Mobile phones are very* **useful**, *especially when you're out shopping.*

handy

practical

convenient

2 *She gave us some very* **useful** *advice.*

helpful

valuable

OPPOSITE **useless**

useless adjective

1 *This old bicycle is* **useless**!

unusable

worthless

OPPOSITE **useful**

2 *I was a* **useless** *goalkeeper.*

hopeless

terrible

incompetent

OPPOSITE **good**

usual adjective

1 *I went to bed at my* **usual** *time of eight o'clock.*

normal

ordinary

2 *The* **usual** *answer is no.*

normal

typical

a
b
c
d
e
f
g
h
i
j
k
l
m
n
o
p
q
r
s
t
u
v
w
x
y
z

A
B
C
D
E
F
G
H
I
J
K
L
M
N
O
P
Q
R
S
T
U
V
W
X
Y
Z

Vv

vague adjective

*He only gave a **vague** description of the dog.*

general

unclear

confused

not very detailed

OPPOSITE **exact**

valuable adjective

*Some of these old coins are quite **valuable**.*

expensive

Use **precious** if something is valuable and important to you: *The jewellery my grandmother gave me is very **precious** to me.*

Use **priceless** if something is so valuable you can't say how much it is worth: *These old paintings are **priceless**.*

OPPOSITE **worthless**

variety noun

1 *There is a **variety** of colours to choose from.*

an assortment

a choice

a mixture

a range

2 *They sell ten different **varieties** of ice cream.*

a type

a sort

a kind

vary verb

*The date of Easter **varies** each year.*

to change

to be different *The date is **different** each year.*

vegetable noun

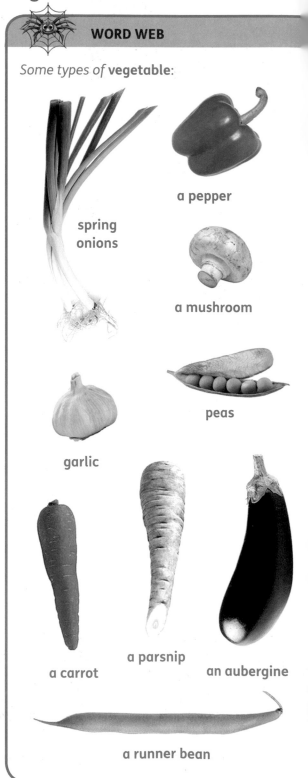

WORD WEB

*Some types of **vegetable**:*

spring onions

a pepper

a mushroom

peas

garlic

a carrot

a parsnip

an aubergine

a runner bean

broccoli

a lettuce

a potato

a courgette

a cucumber

a yam

a beetroot

a squash

an avocado

a leek

spinach

sweetcorn

an onion

celery

a cabbage

a cauliflower

a pumpkin

a b c d e f g h i j k l m n o p q r s t u **v** w x y z

A
B
C
D
E
F
G
H
I
J
K
L
M
N
O
P
Q
R
S
T
U
V
W
X
Y
Z

vibrate verb

*The whole house **vibrates** when a lorry goes past.*

to shake
to wobble
to rattle
to shudder

victory noun

*We celebrated our team's **victory**.*

a win
a success
a triumph
OPPOSITE **defeat**

villain noun

*The police caught the **villain** in the end.*

a criminal
a crook
a baddy

violent adjective

1 *Sometimes the children throw their toys in a **violent** manner.*

aggressive
rough

Use **ferocious** or **savage** if someone is very violent: *She was the victim of a **ferocious** attack.*

2 *That night there was a **violent** storm.*

severe
fierce
raging

visit verb

*I'm going to **visit** my grandma next week.*

to see
to call on
to stay with

visitor noun

*Are you expecting a **visitor** this afternoon?*

a guest
a caller
company *Are you expecting **company**?*

Ww

wait verb

1 Wait *here until I get back.*

to stay

to remain

Use **hang on** or **hold on** when you wait only a short time: **Hang on** *for just a minute. I won't be long.*

2 *She* **waited** *for a while before she opened the door.*

to pause

to hesitate

wake up verb

I **wake up** *at seven o'clock every morning.*

to awaken

to get up

to rise

walk verb

OVERUSED WORD

Here are some more interesting words for **walk**:

They walked *along the street.*

Use **stride** or **march** when someone walks with big steps: *The professor came* **striding** *up to the building.*

Use **hurry** or **rush** when someone walks quickly: *She* **hurried** *down the road to the shop.*

Use **wander**, **stroll**, **amble**, or **saunter** if someone walks slowly: *Matt slowly* **wandered** *over to the door.*

Use **stomp** or **clump** if someone walks noisily: *Tara* **stomped** *angrily out of the room.*

Use **creep**, **sneak**, or **tiptoe** if someone walks very quietly: *I* **crept** *quietly downstairs, trying not to wake anyone.*

Use **limp**, **hobble**, **shuffle**, **stagger**, or **stumble** if someone can't walk very well: *The old man* **hobbled** *along the street.*

Use **trudge** or **plod** if someone walks in a tired way: *Wearily, we* **trudged** *all the way home.*

Use **strut** or **swagger** if someone walks in a very proud way: *I couldn't bear seeing him* **strutting** *about on the stage, so proud of himself!*

Use **hike** or **trek** if someone walks a long way over rough ground: *We spent two weeks* **hiking** *in the mountains.*

a b c d e f g h i j k l m n o p q r s t u v **w** x y z

211

A
B
C
D
E
F
G
H
I
J
K
L
M
N
O
P
Q
R
S
T
U
V
W
X
Y
Z

want verb

1 *Do you* **want** *an ice cream?*

to fancy

to feel like

to need

to desire *(formal)*

Use **be dying for** or **be desperate for** if you want something very badly: *It's so hot! I'm* **desperate** *for a drink!*

Use **wish for**, **long for**, or **yearn for** if you want something badly but do not think you will be able to have it: *She had always* **longed for** *a pony of her own.*

2 *I* **want** *to be a professional dancer.*

to dream of *I* **dream of** *being a professional footballer.*

to set your heart on *I have* **set my heart on** *being a professional footballer.*

warm adjective

1 *The water was* **warm***.*

lukewarm

tepid

2 *It was a lovely* **warm** *day.*

hot

mild

sunny

boiling hot

3 *I was lovely and* **warm** *in my thick coat.*

hot

cosy

snug

4 *We sat down in front of the* **warm** *fire.*

hot

blazing

roaring

OPPOSITE **cold**

warn verb

1 *He* **warned** *us to stay away from the old quarry.*

to advise

to remind

to tell

2 *Someone had* **warned** *the police about the robbery.*

to alert

to tip someone off *(informal)*

3 *This time I will just* **warn** *you. If you do it again, you will be in big trouble.*

to caution

to give someone a warning *This time I will just give* **you a warning***.*

wash verb

1 *Go and* **wash** *your hands.*

to clean

to rinse

2 *You should* **wash** *more often.*

to have a bath

to bath

to have a shower

to shower

3 *I* **washed** *my hair with shampoo.*

to shampoo

4 *I'm going to **wash** the floor.*

to clean
to mop
to scrub
to wipe

waste noun

*Put the **waste** in the bin.*

rubbish
litter
junk
refuse
trash *(American)*
garbage *(American)*

wasteful adjective

*It's **wasteful** to cook more food than you need.*

extravagant
lavish

watch verb

1 *I could feel that someone was **watching** me.*

to look at
to observe

Use **stare at** if you watch someone for a long time: *Ali was **staring at** the ship, trying to see who was on board.*

Use **gaze at** if you are watching something beautiful or interesting: *We **gazed at** the dancers, amazed by their leaps and jumps.*

2 *Will you **watch** my things while I go for a swim?*

to keep an eye on
to look after
to guard
to mind

water noun

1 *Would you like a glass of **water**?*

mineral water
spring water
tap water

2 *We sat by the side of the **water**.*

a lake
a pond
a reservoir
a river
a stream
the sea
the ocean
a brook

WRITING TIPS

Here are some useful words for writing about **water**:

- *The water in the river **flowed** along smoothly.*
- *Water was **pouring** into the boat.*
- *Cold water **gushed** and **splashed** over the rocks.*
- *The water **trickled** and **gurgled** over the pebbles.*
- *A few drops of water were still **dripping** from the tap.*
- *The water of the lake **lapped** against the shore.*

She'd forgotten to turn off the tap when she fetched the bucket of water, and all I can say is that there was ten times as much water on the kitchen floor as there was in the play-house when Lotta was scrubbing. —Astrid Lindgren, *Lotta Says No*

a
b
c
d
e
f
g
h
i
j
k
l
m
n
o
p
q
r
s
t
u
v
w
x
y
z

A B C D E F G H I J K L M N O P Q R S T U V **W** X Y Z

wave verb

1 *She* **waved** *to me from the other side of the field.*

to signal

to gesture

2 *The flags were* **waving** *in the wind.*

to stir

to sway

to flap

to shake

to flutter

3 *He* **waved** *the stick over his head.*

to swing

to brandish

wave noun

We played in the **waves**.

the surf

A **breaker** *is a very big wave:* Huge **breakers** crashed onto the shore.

way noun

1 *Is this the* **way** *to London?*

a road

a route

a direction

a course

a path

a track

2 *This is the best* **way** *to build a den.*

a method *This is the best* **method** *of building a den.*

a technique *This is the best* **technique** *for building a den.*

3 *The teacher spoke in a very nice* **way**.

a manner

a fashion

4 *She ties her hair up in a very pretty* **way**.

a style

weak adjective

1 *She still feels quite* **weak** *after her illness.*

ill

poorly

feeble

frail

shaky

delicate

2 *You're too* **weak** *to fight against me!*

weedy

puny

3 *I think these wooden posts are too* **weak**.

thin

flimsy

fragile

rickety

4 *This orange squash is too* **weak**.

watery

tasteless

diluted

OPPOSITE **strong**

wealthy adjective

Her parents are **wealthy**.

rich

well-off

prosperous

OPPOSITE **poor**

wear verb wears, wearing, wore

1 *He was* **wearing** *a smart blue jacket.*

to have on

to be dressed in

to be sporting

2 *What shall I* **wear** *today?*

to put on

to dress in

weird adjective

*They wear some **weird** clothes!*

strange

funny

peculiar

odd

OPPOSITE **ordinary**

well adjective

*I hope you are **well**.*

fit

healthy

OPPOSITE **ill**

well adverb

1 *You have done this work very **well**.*

carefully

competently

properly

successfully

thoroughly

Use **brilliantly** or **excellently** if you do something very well: *Everyone in our team played **brilliantly**!*

Use **cleverly** or **skilfully** if you do something in a clever way: *He painted **skilfully**.*

OPPOSITE **badly**

2 *They don't treat their pets very **well**.*

kindly

lovingly

caringly

OPPOSITE **badly**

well-known adjective

*He's a very **well-known** pop star.*

famous

celebrated

OPPOSITE **unknown**

went past tense *see* go

wet adjective

1 *My shoes are **wet**.*

Use **damp** if something is slightly wet: *I wiped the table with a **damp** cloth.*

Use **soaked**, **soaking wet**, **dripping wet**, or **drenched** if something is very wet: *My clothes were all **dripping wet** after I fell into the swimming pool!*

2 *The field is too **wet** to play on.*

muddy

soggy

waterlogged

3 *It was a **wet** day.*

rainy

drizzly

showery

damp

OPPOSITE **dry**

whisper verb

*'Which way shall we go?' he **whispered**.*

Use **murmur** if you speak very gently: *'I must be dreaming,' she **murmured**.*

Use **mutter** or **mumble** if you speak quietly and not clearly: *The witch was **muttering** a strange spell to herself.*

Use **hiss** if you speak in a loud or angry whisper: *'Get out of here!' he **hissed**.*

white adjective

*She was wearing a **white** dress.*

cream

ivory

snow white

whole adjective

*We ate the **whole** cake.*

complete

entire

a
b
c
d
e
f
g
h
i
j
k
l
m
n
o
p
q
r
s
t
u
v
w
x
y
z

A B C D E F G H I J K L M N O P Q R S T U V **W** X Y Z

wicked adjective

1 *The land was ruled by a cruel and* **wicked** *king.*

bad

evil

2 *That was a* **wicked** *thing to do.*

wrong

bad

immoral

sinful

OPPOSITE **good**

wide adjective

We had to cross a **wide** *river.*

broad

big

large

OPPOSITE **narrow**

wild adjective

1 *Lions are* **wild** *animals and can be dangerous.*

untamed

ferocious

OPPOSITE **tame**

2 *Their behaviour can be a bit* **wild** *sometimes.*

noisy

rough

boisterous

unruly

rowdy

OPPOSITE **calm**

will verb

1 *I* **will** *tell my teacher tomorrow.*

to intend to *I* **intend to** *tell my teacher tomorrow.*

2 *I* **will** *help you with your homework.*

to be willing to *I am* **willing to** *help you.*

to be happy to *I am* **happy to** *help you.*

willing adjective

Are you **willing** *to help us tomorrow night?*

happy

ready

prepared

eager

keen

inclined

OPPOSITE **unwilling**

win verb wins, winning, won

1 *I was delighted when my team* **won**.

to be victorious

to triumph

to succeed

to come first

to finish first

OPPOSITE **lose**

2 *She* **won** *a medal in the cross-country race.*

to get

to earn

to receive

wind verb (rhymes with *find*)
winds, winding, wound

*She **wound** her scarf round her neck.*

to wrap

to loop

to coil

to twist

wind noun (rhymes with *tinned*)

*Outside, the **wind** was blowing.*

A **breeze** is a gentle wind: *It was a hot day, but there was a lovely cool **breeze**.*

A **gale** is a strong wind: *We couldn't play outside because there was a **gale** blowing.*

A **hurricane** is a very strong wind: *A lot of houses were damaged by the **hurricane**.*

WRITING TIPS

Here are some useful words for writing about the **wind**:

- *A gentle wind was **blowing** across the field.*
- *The **strong** wind **howled** and **roared** and **whistled** through the trees.*
- *The **terrible** wind **buffeted** the small boats on the lake.*

windy adjective

*It was a cold, **windy** night.*

breezy

blustery

stormy

OPPOSITE **calm**

winner noun

*James is the **winner**!*

the champion

the victor

OPPOSITE **loser**

wipe verb

1 *I'll **wipe** the table before we eat.*

to clean

2 *She used a duster to **wipe** the furniture.*

to dust

to polish

3 *Please could you **wipe** the mud off your shoes?*

to rub

to scrape

wise adjective

1 *My grandfather is a very **wise** man.*

clever

intelligent

sensible

2 *You have made a **wise** decision.*

good

sensible

OPPOSITE **foolish**

wish verb

*I had always **wished** for a puppy.*

to want

to long for

to yearn for

a
b
c
d
e
f
g
h
i
j
k
l
m
n
o
p
q
r
s
t
u
v
w
x
y
z

217

A B C D E F G H I J K L M N O P Q R S T U V **W** X Y Z

witch noun
a sorceress
an enchantress

wizard noun
a sorcerer
an enchanter
a magician

wobble verb
1 *The ladder* **wobbled** *as I climbed up it.*
to shake
to sway
to be unsteady
2 *The jelly* **wobbles** *when you move the plate.*
to shake
to quiver

woman noun
What was the **woman's** *name?*
a lady
a girl
a **mother** a woman who has children
a **widow** a woman whose husband has died

won verb past tense *see* win

wonder noun
We stared at the lights in **wonder**.
amazement
admiration
awe

wonder verb
I was **wondering** *what to do next.*
to think about
to consider

wonderful adjective
We had a **wonderful** *time at the park.*
great
amazing
brilliant
fantastic
marvellous
OPPOSITE **terrible**

wood noun
1 *Our garden shed is made of* **wood**.
timber
planks
2 *We need more* **wood** *for the fire.*
logs
3 *We walked through the* **wood**.
woods
woodland
A **forest** is a large wood: *They were scared to go into the huge, dark* **forest**.
A **copse** is a very small wood: *We found a picnic spot near a little* **copse**.

wore verb past tense *see* wear

work noun
1 *We were told to sit quietly and get on with our* **work**.
a job
schoolwork
homework
a task

2 *What* **work** *do you want to do when you grow up?*
a job
an occupation
a profession
a career
3 *The* **work** *can be back-breaking.*
labour
toil

work verb

1 *We* **worked** *hard all morning.*
to be busy *We were* **busy** *all morning.*
to toil
to labour
2 *When I grow up I want to* **work** *in a bank.*
to be employed
to have a job
3 *The lift isn't* **working**.
to go *The lift doesn't* **go**.
to function *The lift isn't* **functioning**.
4 *I don't think your plan will* **work**.
to succeed
to be successful

worried adjective

1 *I was* **worried** *because they were so late.*
anxious
concerned
2 *Are you* **worried** *about moving to a new school?*
nervous
apprehensive
OPPOSITE **relaxed**

worry verb

Don't **worry**, *everything will be all right.*
to fret
to be anxious
to be concerned

worry noun

I seem to have so many **worries** *at the moment.*
a concern
a fear

wound noun (rhymes with *spooned*)

He had a nasty **wound** *on his arm.*
an injury
a cut
a gash

wound verb

The explosion **wounded** *a lot of people.*
to injure
to hurt

wound verb past tense *see* wind

wrap verb

1 *I* **wrapped** *the parcel in paper.*
to cover
to pack
2 *I* **wrapped** *my scarf round my neck.*
to wind
to loop

wreck verb

1 *The explosion* **wrecked** *several buildings.*
to destroy
to demolish
to smash up
2 *He drove into a lamppost and* **wrecked** *his car.*
to smash up
3 *You've* **wrecked** *my DVD player!*
to break
to ruin
to smash

a b c d e f g h i j k l m n o p q r s t u v **w** x y z

A B C D E F G H I J K L M N O P Q R S T U V **W** X Y Z

write verb writes, writing, wrote

1 *He* **wrote** *the word 'birthday' at the top of the page.*

Use **print** when you write something without the letters joined up: *He* **printed** *each word carefully in capital letters.*

Use **jot down** when you write something quickly: *I quickly* **jotted down** *her phone number.*

Use **scribble** or **scrawl** when you write something messily: *I* **scribbled** *a quick message to the others.*

2 *Please* **write** *your name here.*
to sign

3 *I* **wrote** *a list of all the things we would need.*
to compile
to make

4 *I enjoy* **writing** *stories.*
to make up
to tweet
to blog

5 *We're going to* **write** *a piece of music.*
to compose
to create

writer noun

I want to be a **writer** *when I grow up.*
an author

wrong adjective

1 *The information that he gave us was* **wrong**.
false
inaccurate
untrue
incorrect

2 *I thought I would not like eating broccoli, but I was* **wrong**!
mistaken

3 *It is* **wrong** *to steal.*
dishonest
immoral
bad
wicked
OPPOSITE **right**

wrote verb past tense *see* write

 WORD WEB

Some types of **writer**:

an author someone who writes books

a blogger someone who writes their own blog on the Internet

a journalist someone who writes for a newspaper

a playwright someone who writes plays

a poet

a scriptwriter someone who writes scripts for films

a tweeter someone who writes short messages about what they are doing on a website

Yy

yell verb
*The man **yelled** at us to go away.*

to shout
to scream
to shriek
to bawl
to bellow

yellow adjective
*The bridesmaids wore **yellow** dresses.*

lemon
gold
primrose

young adjective
1 *I was too **young** to understand what was happening.*

little
small

Use **immature** or **childish** when someone behaves in a way that seems too young: *Stop being so **childish**!*

OPPOSITE old

2 *My dad is 40, but he still looks quite **young**.*

youthful

OPPOSITE old

Zz

zap verb
*You have to **zap** aliens in this game.*

to kill
to shoot
to destroy
to blast
to hit

zero noun
1 *The temperature went down to **zero**.*

nought
nothing

2 *The other team won by three goals to **zero**.*

nil

zoom verb
*The car **zoomed** along the road.*

to speed
to race
to tear
to hurtle

a
b
c
d
e
f
g
h
i
j
k
l
m
n
o
p
q
r
s
t
u
v
w
x
y
z

Become a Word Explorer!

Contents

Word building

Have you ever thought about making up a word? If there isn't an exact word to describe something, you could try creating your own by thinking what it looks, smells, or tastes like and then adding one of these endings.

| -y | *a fishy smell, an orangey colour, a chocolatey taste* |
| -like | *a snake-like creature, a giraffe-like neck, a silk-like cloth* |

You can also make new words to describe what something looks, smells, or tastes like using these endings:

-looking	*a strange-looking man, a fierce-looking dog*
-smelling	*sweet-smelling perfume, disgusting-smelling socks*
-tasting	*delicious-tasting soup, foul-tasting medicine*

Example:

If you are describing an **ogre**, you could write:

*He had thick **leathery** skin and huge **shark-like** teeth. His eyes were small and **evil-looking**, and from his mouth came **foul-smelling** breath.*

Similes

Similes are comparisons using '**as**' or '**like**'. They can liven up your writing and of course, you can make up your own!

Here are similes using 'as':

blind **as** a bat   good **as** gold

clear **as** a bell   hard **as** nails

clear **as** mud   light **as** a feather

cunning **as** a fox   quiet **as** a mouse

dry **as** a bone   strong **as** an ox

fit **as** a fiddle

Here are similes using 'like':

built **like** a tank   memory **like** an elephant

chatter **like** a monkey   move **like** a snail

eyes **like** a hawk   sing **like** a bird

fits **like** a glove   swim **like** a fish

fight **like** cats and dogs

Collective nouns

Collective nouns are words that are used to talk about groups of things, usually animals. There is often more than one way to refer to the groups, but some common examples include:

an **army** of caterpillars, frogs

a **band** of gorillas

a **brood** of chickens

a **colony** of ants, rabbits, beavers

a **flock** of sheep, birds

a **gaggle** of geese

a **herd** of horses, cows, goats, yaks, llamas, hippopotamuses

a **litter** of puppies, kittens, cubs

a **murder** of crows

a **nest** of snakes

a **pack** of wolves, polar bears

a **pod** of walruses, seals, dolphins, whales

a **pride** of lions

a **school** of sharks, salmon, whales

a **shoal** of fish

a **troop** of monkeys, kangaroos

a **swarm** of bees, insects

an **unkindness** of ravens

Writing stories

TOP TEN TIPS

Before you write:

1. Plan your story carefully—something must happen in a story.

2. Tell your story to a friend before you write. Would you want to read this story? Would your friend? Change your plan if necessary.

While you are writing:

3. Keep to your new plan when you write. Now is not a good time to change your mind.

4. Write in sentences and think about punctuation.

5. Don't forget paragraphs. If you need to begin a sentence with an adverbial clause of time (e.g. Later that day... When it was all over...) or place (e.g. Outside, in the woods...) you probably need to start a new paragraph.

After you have written the first draft:

6. Use your **Oxford Junior Illustrated Thesaurus** to check your spelling.

7. Use this thesaurus to make sure you have chosen the best words.

8. Look at the Overused words list. Try to use other words.

9. Can you add in some details about your characters to make your reader interested and want to know more about the characters?

10. Can you add more information about your setting to help your reader to 'see' it in their mind?

Creating a setting: Place

The first thing you must decide is where your story takes place.

Is it in a **forest** or on a **beach**? Is it in a **castle** or in a **house?** Is it at **sea** or on an **island**?

Once you have chosen your setting, try to picture it in your mind and then describe all the details to your reader.

For example, are there **mountains** or **trees**? Are there **people** or **animals**?

Every time you add a detail, try to add an adjective to describe it.

Example:

If you are describing a forest you could write:

*All around us there were **massive**, **ancient oak** trees, with **thick trunks** and **dense**, **dark-green leaves**.*

EXPLORER TIP

Don't worry if you can't think of a good adjective straight away. Look up a common adjective, such as **big**, **small**, **old**, or **new** and then choose a more interesting and unusual synonym.

Creating a setting: Time

You need to tell your readers when the things happen in your story. What happens first? What happens next?

Try to use these time words and phrases to make it clear when things happen.

What happened next

Later that day, *we arrived in London.*

The next morning *we set out again.*

Eventually, *we managed to open the door.*

What happened earlier

*Mika had left **a few minutes earlier**.*

***A moment before**, he had seen something moving in the bushes.*

***Earlier that day**, Sammy had phoned.*

What happened at the same time

***Meanwhile**, the others were still waiting at home.*

***At that very moment**, Carla was getting on the train.*

Just as *I was leaving, I heard a tap on the window.*

As soon as *I saw him, I recognized him.*

Creating a setting: Atmosphere

When you describe the setting of your story, think about the mood of the story. Choose your words carefully to create your atmosphere.

Does the place seem **happy** and **cheerful**?
Is it **dark**, **gloomy,** and **frightening**?
Does it feel **friendly**, or is it **quiet** and **lonely**?

You can also describe the weather to match the atmosphere of your story. If your story is happy, it can be **bright** and **sunny**, but if your story is frightening, the weather could be **dark** and **stormy**.

Example:

For a **gloomy** or **frightening** atmosphere, you might write:

As Max approached the ***dark, deserted*** *castle, a* ***bitter*** *wind* ***whistled*** *through the pine trees.*

EXPLORER TIP

Try looking up the words **hot** and **cold** to find words to describe the weather. You can also look up words such as **wind** and **rain** to find lots of different words you can use.

Creating a character

To write good stories, you must create interesting characters. First think about your character's appearance.

Is your character **short** or **tall**? Are they **fat** or **thin**?
Is their hair **long** and **straight** or **short** and **curly**?

Then think about their personality.

Are they **kind** and **good-natured**?
Or are they **bad-tempered** and **mean?**
Think of three or four interesting adjectives to create a lively picture of your character.

Example:

If you are describing a **kind old man**, you might write:

Old Mr Brown was ***short*** *and rather* ***plump***. *He always seemed to be* ***cheerful*** *and* ***good-humoured***, *and* ***beamed*** *at everyone when he spoke.*

EXPLORER TIP

Try looking up common adjectives such as **fat**, **thin**, **happy**, and **grumpy** to find some interesting words for describing characters.

Describing action

When you are describing what happens in your story, try to use words which describe exactly how someone does something.

For example, does someone **march in to the room**, **creep downstairs**, **stroll along the beach**, or **trudge home**?

Example:

If you are writing about a person **running**, you might write:

*Tom **raced** home as fast as he could and **dashed** upstairs to his room.*

If you are writing about an animal, you might write:

*Little birds were **twittering** in the trees above me, then one **fluttered** down and landed by my foot.*

EXPLORER TIP

Look at the panels for **go**, **run**, and **walk** to find lots of different ways of saying how someone moves. Look up the panels at words such as **car**, **boat**, **dog**, **cat** and **bird** for specific action words to describe these things.

Writing dialogue

The words that your characters say in your story are the dialogue. When you are writing dialogue, remember to use speech marks correctly and try to use different words for reporting what your characters say.

Think about what your character is saying.

Are they **asking a question**, **giving an answer**, or **making a suggestion**? Think about how they speak. Do they speak in a **loud**, **angry voice**, or a **quiet voice**?

Example:

If someone is asking a **question**, you might write:

*'Do you live near here?' **she enquired.***

*'How old are you?' **she asked.***

If someone speaks in a **loud**, **angry voice** you might write:

*'You fool!' **yelled** Matt.*

*'Go away!' she **snapped.***

EXPLORER TIP

Look up the word panel at **say** to find lots of interesting words you can use. You can also look at the examples there to check how to use the speech marks correctly.

227

Writing non-fiction

When you are writing non-fiction, it is important to think about **who** you are writing it for and **why** you are writing it.

Is it a **newspaper report** to describe something that happened, or is it an **advertisement** to persuade people to buy something? If you are writing a newspaper report, choose words to make it interesting and accurate. If you are writing an advertisement, choose words to persuade people that something is good.

Example:

In a **newspaper report** of a robbery, you might write:

*The thief **assaulted** Mrs Edwards in the street and tried to **snatch** her bag. He has now been **captured** by the police.*

In an advertisement, you might write:

*This **brand-new, cut-price** phone has **loads** of **fantastic** features. Buy one today!*

EXPLORER TIP

Write a draft of your text first, then go through it and underline the common adjectives and verbs that you have used. Look these up in the thesaurus to see if you can find some more interesting, accurate, or persuasive ones!

We write **letters**, **emails**, and **texts** to different people and for different purposes.

Before you write, you need to think about who you are writing to (your **audience**) and why you are writing (your **purpose**).

The following are examples of letters written to one person during a day. Think about who they are to, and why they are written.

Writing a text message

03/06   15:23 ✉

JEN, C U L8R.
PARK.5ISH.
LOL. xx

LOOK OUT FOR

- the use of abbreviations
- the use of letters to take the place of words
- no sentences
- very informal tone

Writing a thank you letter

Dear Aunty Jen,

Thank you for the pens you sent me for my birthday. I took them into school and everyone said that you must be the best to send me a pressy like that! I am working hard because we have a maths test next week. I hate tests but I know that I feel better if I do well. Wish me luck!

Thanks again for the pens.

Lots of love,

Sarah

LOOK OUT FOR

- the salutation *(Dear Aunty Jen)*
- the introduction of the subject early in the letter *(thank you for)*
- information about the writer
- the use of slang *(pressy, you must be the best)*
- use of exclamation marks
- information about the writer *(in school – we know it's a child)*
- informal tone

Writing a formal invitation

Mrs J Davies

Mr and Mrs E Jones invite you to attend the wedding of their daughter

Elizabeth

to

Jay Singh

The wedding will take place at The Palace Hotel , Northington on 23rd February at 3.30 p.m.

RSVP

LOOK OUT FOR

- the salutation *(Mrs J Davis)*
- the early introduction about the purpose of the letter
- the information needed for the invitation to be successful
- tell the events as they will happen
- RSVP *(respondez s'il vous plait is a formal French way of asking someone to reply)*
- very formal tone

Dear Mrs Davies,

I understand you are responsible for cooking the fudge in Ye Old Sweet Shoppe. On the afternoon of 23rd November, I was passing the shop and I was attracted to the smell of your cooking. I came into the shop and, unfortunately, bought a bag of the fudge. I ate the entire contents of the bag within ten minutes. That evening I found that I had put on a whole kilo in weight when I am on a diet and trying to LOSE weight. I hold you entirely responsible for my weight gain. It is thoughtless of you to leave the shop door open while you are cooking as the smell is inevitably going to tempt passers-by into your shop. I assume that you will now take steps to ensure that it doesn't happen again.

Yours sincerely,

Ethel Smith

Mrs Ethel Smith

LOOK OUT FOR

- the salutation (*Dear Mrs Davis*)
- the introduction of the subject early in the letter
- information about the complaint
- the expectation that the complaint will be sorted out
- signing off with *Yours sincerely*
- formal tone